3-1-71

ROAD RACING IN AMERICA

ROAD RACING

Produced by Lyle Kenyon Engel

IN AMERICA

and the editors of Auto Racing *Magazine*

Dodd, Mead & Company, New York

*IN MEMORY OF GEORGE WEAVER
AND WALT HANSGEN WHO SET THE
HIGHEST STANDARDS FOR ROAD
RACERS OF AMERICA*

Thanks are due *Sports Car Graphic* for permission to use material in Chapter 2 previously published in its pages.

Thanks are owed also to the Sports Car Club of America and its public relations director, Dic Van der Feen, for assistance with many aspects of this book, and especially for material appearing in Chapters 1, 4, 9 and 10.

1579898

EDITORIAL STAFF

Karl Ludvigsen   George Engel   Marla Ray

PHOTOGRAPHERS

Jack Atkins	George Engel	David Phipps
Major W. Baynes	Lyle Kenyon Engel	John Plow
Kenneth H. Coles	L. I. Feuerhelm	Gerald Schmitt
Arnie de Brier	Fourscore Associates	Judy Stropus
Eric della Faille	Karl Ludvigsen	Dennis Torres
Beverly Engel	Pete Lyons	George Wintersteen

INTRODUCTION

I'm not sure what caused it. The machines are fascinating, to be sure, intricately conceived and superbly balanced devices for consuming pavement—any pavement, of any shape—as rapidly as possible. There are the places, too, the glamour of Monte Carlo, Le Mans, Mille Miglia, Reims and Nürburgring. Then there are the men like Juan Manuel Fangio, Alberto Ascari, Jean Pierre Wimille, Nino Farina, Stirling Moss and Mike Hawthorn. The cars, the tracks, the men, the atmosphere, the history extending from the dawn of the century—not one but all of these are to blame for making me a faithful fan of road racing.

There had been road racing in America during the early years of the Twentieth Century, as you'll learn in the pages to follow. But during the two decades between the Great Wars it was, if not dead, at least dormant. Creation of the Indianapolis Motor Speedway had focused the attention of both the public and the manufacturers on sheer speed rather than the variety of road racing. In 1921 we were still building a car, the Duesenberg, good enough to go to Europe and win a Grand Prix race there. Not until 1967 did this happen again.

Our rough roads of those years of growth, and our need for reliable cars and lots of them, led to the development of tough, cheap, good-riding automobiles. There wasn't much concern for handling and braking, and the industry didn't have time to tool down to smaller quantities to make a specialty-type sports car. Writing about an American road race meeting in 1937, the correspondent of Britain's *Speed* noted that "not one stock car made in the country is suitable for racing, and that therefore all the cars they drive have to be shipped from abroad and, more important still, all spare parts are equally difficult to obtain." Come to think of it, things haven't changed all that much!

The race meeting *Speed* wrote about took place at Long Island's Roosevelt Raceway and was organized by the Automobile Racing Club of America. Tracing its origins to 1929, this tiny band of enthusiasts along the New York-New England axis raced first on miniature private tracks and then, for the first time in 1934, on normal roads closed for the occasion. Men who were to help the sport back to its feet with the SCCA after World War II had already been active in ARCA days: Sam and Miles Collier, George Rand, George Weaver, Al Garthwaite and George Huntoon were among them.

In those days there were no road circuits in America built for that purpose alone. Never very satisfactory, Roosevelt Raceway had folded after 1937. By 1951, when I first saw a road race, at Watkins Glen, events had been held either on airports (Santa Ana, Suffolk, Sebring, Palm Springs) or on public roads closed for the races (Pebble Beach, Elkhart Lake, Watkins Glen, Bridgehampton, Palm Beach, Reno).

The 6.6-mile course at Watkins Glen was incredible, in retrospect, with its precipitous climbs and descents, its oiled dirt sections and its no-passing zone through the railroad underpass. Phil Walters, the imperturbable former midget driver, won with style in his white C-2 Cunningham. George Weaver was a dual winner, in the "Unrestricted" event with his Grand Prix V8 Maserati and in the under-1500cc class with a rare Le Mans Jowett Jupiter. Downtown that weekend the Glen was swarming with the most interesting cars in America, from Allards, Duesenbergs, Lagondas and Bugattis to GM's new Le Sabre.

Next year everything was set for the greatest-ever Glen race in 1952. But crowd control around the vast circuit was almost nonexistent, delaying the first two races. When the main event was flagged off, disaster was not far away. A Dan Rubin photograph records, frozen for all time, the moment after Fred Wacker's Allard swings wide to the left at the end of Franklin Street, caroming off the curb, leaving behind one school child mortally hurt, others wounded. Behind, John Fitch swerves his Cunningham away from the scene while he looks back at the spectators, picnic lunches and folding chairs scattered along the sidewalk. The race was red-flagged to a halt.

This looked, for a while, like the end of the renaissance of road racing in America. New York barred racing on state roads, sending the Glen events to a new network of country roads. Wisconsin did the same, halting the Elkhart Lake races after 1952. Bridgehampton had a Glen-like tragedy in 1953. The Strategic Air Command came to the rescue, providing both airports and personnel in 1953 and '54 for the major national road races. This gave much-needed breathing time, time for planning and construction of new private tracks at Bridgehampton, Thompson, Elkhart, Lime Rock, Riverside, Marlboro and Continental Divide. Typically these first-generation road circuits were built and financed by enthusiasts, and sometimes operated by them too, which wasn't necessarily the best arrangement.

That's the way it went for another ten years, until professionals found out there was money to be made in presenting and promoting road races, building new tracks and developing television coverage to elevate the sport to the high level of appreciation and attendance it enjoys today. In fact, as the costs of road racing spiral upward, many feel the sport will be able to bloom fully only in the United States.

There were many important milestones along this road to success. One was the inclusion of the Sebring 12-Hour Race among those counting for championship points in 1953 (or maybe 1954; see Chapter 2). Another was the staging of the first modern United States Grand Prix in 1959, followed by the crowning in 1961 of our first World Champion Driver, Phil Hill. Also symbolic of America's commitment to road racing were the major efforts to build cars by Briggs Cunningham, Lance Reventlow (Scarab), Jim Hall (Chaparral), Ford Motor Company and Dan Gurney (AAR Eagle). They've shown the world we can create the cars as well as the tracks and drivers.

The assembly of the Can-Am series, and then the Trans-Am, marked other big steps forward in American road racing. Another will come when a second World Championship Grand Prix race is established in America, probably in California. But that won't be a very interesting race if there are no American drivers in it, and the way we're going that could easily happen.

Early in the Sixties it seemed that American drivers were on their way to prominence in world road racing. After Phil Hill, both Dan Gurney and Richie Ginther showed they could win Grand Prix races, the highest and toughest-fought level of road racing. Also Walt Hansgen, Jim Hall and Ronnie Bucknum demonstrated they could collect Championship points in Grand Prix events. Walt is no longer with us, and the rest have either retired from racing or decided to concentrate on the richer racing of North America. As the Seventies opened only Mario Andretti was flying the American banner abroad, just above the STP pennant.

We couldn't do much better than Mario. But many abroad are quick to claim he's more Italian than American! If our racing schools are so good, in other words, and our club and professional road racing series so competitive and widespread, why haven't we sent more American drivers to the top of the road-racing profession? I think we will, in time, if our manufacturers should take more direct interest in Grand Prix competition. Meanwhile one road racing group is considering a move that would certainly help: lowering from twenty-one to eighteen the age at which you're allowed to start racing. You must, today, start early.

It's not easy to understand, this sport. There are many classes, many kinds of races, many different factors that affect the performance of a combination of car and driver. It's not simple, but that's why road racing is so interesting. And that's why this book was written about it.

KARL LUDVIGSEN

Pelham Manor, New York

CONTENTS

Thundering into one of road racing's tight turns on the way to victory are the Chevrolet Corvettes of Jerry Thompson (6) and Tony DeLorenzo (1). The Owens-Corning Fiberglas Racing Team competes in SCCA's Central Division A-Production events.

1 YOUR SPORTS CAR ON THE TRACK

You've seen him around town, though you may not have thought about it. You know he works in an office, maybe a clerk, a lawyer or and ad man, but you've noticed he can't seem to keep his fingernails clean. For a while he was driving one of those little sports cars to work—an MG or Alfa or Triumph, something like that—but now when you go by his house you see it in the garage, jacked up, big tubes sticking out of the cockpit. The family station wagon is in the driveway, and when his wife is parked at the supermarket you notice its trailer hitch and stickers on the windshield marked "PADDOCK."

What does it all mean? It means he's discovered an absorbing hobby that showed him how to pack a week's worth of fun, work, excitement and satisfaction into a two-day weekend. He's found out that the sports car he bought to drive to work was actually a racing car in disguise, designed that way by the people who made it, who knew that a real sports car should be able to race as well as run errands. And it wasn't all that difficult to make it into a racing car, one that could still be driven on the street.

That neighbor of yours is one of the thousands of Americans who found out there was such a thing as sports car road racing, then realized that it could be fun to watch but even more fun to take part. He probably started by reading about it, by buying a copy of *Road & Track* or *Auto Racing* or *Sports Car Graphic*. Then he might have checked the column on auto racing in his local paper to find out what was going on that weekend. Chances are there were some road races listed because many of the nearly 100 road circuits throughout the United States have something scheduled almost every weekend. The leading national road racing organization sanctioned 339 different competition weekends in 1969.

Once bitten by the bug, our budding road-racing enthusiast probably didn't plunge directly into car-to-car competition. He might instead have located one of the thousands of "solo" events that are run each year on the vast parking lots of shopping centers, public parks and industrial centers of the U.S. Depending on where you live, such an event may be known as an "autocross," "slalom" or "gymkhana."

Because these closed-course, time-and-maneuverability events place a greater emphasis on precision and skill than speed, and on the participant rather than the spectator, they are relatively safe, inexpensive and the best form of driver education available anywhere. By definition, they are "one car at a time" events: one car against the clock.

In its present and most popular form an autocross course bears a faint resemblance to a road race circuit. The sharpness of the left- and right-hand turns and the trickiness of the required maneuvers are at the discretion of the organizers.

Because of the usually limited space the temporary course is laid out in such a manner that speeds are held to a minimum. Total

2

Jim Dittemore's Triumph TR6 (8) leads a Porsche 911
in SCCA's C- Production class.

course length rarely reaches one mile. The driver has to negotiate
"gates" laid out with rubber pylons that border a twisting, turning
route. And the pylons are placed close together, often with no more
than a few inches clearance for the car as it passes through. The end
of the route is close to the starting mark, forming a circuit.

The payoff in an autocross is for precision. The over-enthusiastic
driver who gaily clouts pylons hither and yon will be penalized
valuable seconds.

An autocross is normally run in a fairly straightforward manner.
A car is timed and scored on a run of one lap at a time around the
serpentine course. The driver is not required to stop or back up and
the course is laid out in such a fashion that he will seldom get above
second gear.

A variation on the autocross is called the "gymkhana," actually
the event from which the modern autocross evolved. The gymkhana

usually combines the precision at moderate speeds of the autocross with activities related to everyday driving and a few gimmicks thrown in just for fun. Some gymkhana events have competitors backing into "garages" laid out with pylons, parking parallel, breaking balloons with pointed sticks and executing a variety of other happenings.

Autocrosses provide some of the thrills and lessons of racing for drivers who cannot or do not race. Racing can be very expensive and darned hard work. For better or for worse, the vast majority of sporting drivers do not race and never will. But the motor sport exponent can fulfill his Dan Gurney fantasies in the Sunday afternoon autocross with negligible risk of life, limb, pocketbook and domestic tranquility.

With wives as well as husbands able to take part, there is no need for an "autocross widow." While the golfer's mate might be home cursing her fate on Sunday afternoon, the autocross spouse is more likely to be holding a watch on the old man to see if he can beat her time.

As a matter of fact, unacknowledged by the men, the whole road racing sport would come to a stop without the girls. Numerous duties involved in race participation and organization can be and often are best performed by women, not the least appealing or essential of which is Permanent Number One Member of some lucky man's pit crew.

The team member in slacks usually plays an essential role in timing her hero, errand-going, packing, and driving the whole station-wagon-plus-trailer-with-race-car home Sunday night for the male achiever flaked out in the right-hand seat.

The ladies' handling of race personnel registration as well as their having charge of the work attendant on race entries have made the two vital functions female preserves throughout the country. And you get to meet everyone.

Similarly, women make excellent timers and scorers for race events. No serious competition can take place without these two specialties capably staffed. The overwhelming majority of race timers and scorers are women, many of them with formal specialty licenses.

As a driver, car owner, scorer or worker around the race track, our enthusiast will find that he or she will be interested in joining one of the clubs active in road racing. Again, the local paper's events listings will identify the clubs that are staging various events. Large companies and schools usually have clubs of their own. The owner of a Porsche, Alfa Romeo, Jaguar, Mercedes-Benz, Lancia, Corvette or Triumph—among others—will find active national clubs catering to activities for those makes. They stress the social side, too, which mustn't be overlooked.

Many regional sports car clubs have enough know-how and personnel to conduct their own car-against-car racing events. But the dominant organization in the field, one that's made some good moves in its more than twenty-five years to consolidate its position, is the Sports Car Club of America, Inc. (SCCA). This not-for-profit club conducts more races than any other single racing organization in the world. It also sanctions more International races than any U.S. club, including all the World Championship races held in America.

With the help and supervision of its member-volunteers, in 1970 SCCA conducted 2000 separate races, involving 5500 specially licensed drivers at 100 sites. This broadly based program of competition provides racing opportunities for at least forty classes of sports cars, Grand Touring cars, formula cars and small sedans. And competition ranges from low-pressure regional club racing to the most intense factory team contention. Paid spectator admissions at SCCA races in 1969 numbered 1.4 million. Total attendance at events was probably double that.

Chartered by the national SCCA organization are 104 semi-autonomous regions, whose territory covers the fifty United States. Each member of the SCCA holds dual membership, in the national organization and his home region. Each region elects its own volunteer officers, conducts a wide variety of sports car events in its locality and holds regular membership meetings. The regions operate independently within the overall national framework. The regions are banded together into seven divisions for competitive purposes and into eleven areas for administrative purposes.

The management and overall policy for the club is determined by a board of governors elected by the membership from each of the areas. The governors are assisted by members appointed to a dozen boards and committees to administer various club affairs and make recommendations to the governors. There are also close-to-the-scene officials in each division to supervise competition.

Because it is member-oriented and member-operated, the club stresses participation on a broad basis. The over-100 national and divisional officers and committeemen come from all walks of life and all parts of the country, as do all the members. Their position in the club is based both on their ability to serve the members and their deep interest in maintaining and improving the sport. This is reflected in the growth of the SCCA since 1944 from a club of just seven avid originators to its present size of 18,500 members, who have found the fun of participating in every facet of automotive sport.

The easiest way to get more information on the SCCA is to send for the Club's "$5 Kit," a package containing all the material you could ask for on racing, rallying, competition rules and Club programs. To get it, send five bucks to the SCCA, P.O. Box 791, Westport, Connecticut 06880, and ask them for the Kit. You may also want to write for information to some other organizations that, as you'll see in later chapters, are also in the road racing business. One is the United States Auto Club, P.O. Box 24001, Speedway, Indiana 46224, and another is the International Motor Sports Association, P.O. Box 805, Fairfield, Connecticut 06430.

Several of these clubs are also affiliated with the rest of the racing world through the Automobile Competition Committee for the United States, FIA, Inc. ACCUS is a non-stock, non-profit organization which was founded in 1957 and incorporated in 1960. It is the permanent representative of all American international motor sports and is headquartered at 433 Main Street, Stamford, Connecticut 06901.

ACCUS is composed of fourteen individual members and four club members.

Japanese Datsuns, German Porsches and British Triumphs battle each other in SCCA's C-Production class. These are factory racing teams, competing for trophies.

The individual members consist of six of the original founders of the committee and two delegate members proposed by each of the four member clubs: The National Association for Stock Car Auto Racing, the National Hot Rod Association, The Sports Car Club of America and the United States Auto Club.

ACCUS is the American representative of the International Sporting Committee, known in French as the Commission Sportive Internationale, or CSI, one department of the Fédération Internationale de l'Automobile (FIA), based in Paris, France.

The FIA, founded in 1904, is a voluntary association of the national automobile clubs of approximately seventy countries. Its purposes are to encourage and promote international exchange of ideas, customs, cars, technical information and motor sports. The CSI is the organization actually responsible for the conduct of international motor sport. The other department of the FIA is the International Technical, Touring & Traffic Section, to which the AAA is the American representative.

The CSI is made up of delegates from twelve countries, among which the five great manufacturing nations of England, France, Germany, Italy and the United States are permanent members. The remaining seven are elected annually from the ranks of the remaining FIA member countries.

Once our enthusiastic friend joined a road racing club, a whole new world opened up to him. He faced a fantastic new vocabulary of performance classifications, tech inspections, sanctions, entry fees, homologation and disqualification. But he also found that all these terms were well explained and, generally, wisely applied. The SCCA's general competition rules (GCR) occupy 160 pages today, compared to only twenty-four in the late Fifties. Their greater complexity is the result of both experience and the fabulous growth that road racing has enjoyed. The number of road racing events sanctioned (approved and supervised) by the SCCA tripled from 1955 to 1960 and tripled again by 1970.

Much of the appeal of road racing lies in its challenge and variety. Road courses provide both left and right turns which can be driven at speeds ranging from 20 to 120 miles per hour. In racing

Lee Mueller (3) pushes his Triumph Spitfire past two E-Production cars on his way to winning the F-Production class (a slower class than E) in SCCA's national championship events.

parlance these are called "corners" whether they are 180-degree hairpins or flat-out arcs, and each corner has a theoretical maximum speed at which it can be negotiated in any given car. Road courses also rise and fall with the topography and on some tracks elevation changes are extreme and abrupt.

Getting around a road course quickly demands a very capable car. It has to be small and responsive with tremendous stopping power. Tires and suspension must be designed to give it fantastic road holding and it must have a gearbox which will let the engine operate near its maximum power for every speed demanded by the road.

To drive through the corners at their maximum speeds, the driver has to race the road itself, judging how fast he can go into the corner without sliding off. He must select the path or "line" through each corner that will be the fastest, but he also has to keep in mind his position and speed coming out of it for the next corner. And he has to do it lap after lap. Changing gear twenty times just to complete one lap is not at all unusual.

The cars race against each other, but the top drivers compete mainly against the course, trying to shave a tenth of a second here and there, reducing their lap time to one that will eventually put them ahead of the opposition. To do this perfectly every lap involves many driving skills which take time and training to achieve.

But there are many different kinds of cars that can be used in road racing, and there would be little interest or attraction for either driver or spectator if they were all mixed together regardless of their performance abilities. We started out in the late Forties handling this very simply: dividing all the cars into two categories, over and under 1500cc (91 ci). Then for a while the stock MG Race became a fixture of road racing cards because there were so many of these little roadsters around. But MG spoiled that by introducing the TD Mark II and later the 1500cc TF, not to mention the first MGA.

Next the "production" cars were given eleven different displacement classifications from A through K, and similar categories were set up for the "modified" cars, which consisted of anything that

Carl Swanson's GT6+ Triumph wards off threats from

wasn't "production." This system inevitably meant that at any given time one or two cars would be outstandingly good in a certain class. The California Sports Car Club, which later became an SCCA region, countered this by creating "performance classifications" for production sports cars.

At first the "performance" yardstick seemed arbitrary and open to too much argument. It left it to the club to set up eight classes and fit into each one the cars that were chosen in actual lap-time capability. But even in its early stages it made for so much better racing that it was worth the problems of administration. It worked for the Cal Club and was later adopted by the SCCA, which is the only road racing group in the world to have such a broad-based

two Alfa Romeo Duettos in SCCA's E-Production class.

production car program and to use this system to make it work.

One more change brought production sports car racing to its present close-fought status. "Production" originally meant just that, only normal replacement parts and pieces listed as optional by the factories being permissible. This led to more spectacular and costly lists of questionable options, with each manufacturer trying to out-option the others. This was halted by the seemingly revolutionary means of loosening up the rules on certain hard-to-restrict parts like pistons and camshafts, and at the same time tightening up on the basic production eligibility.

Each year, of course, the classifications are adjusted to reflect the previous season's performances and to fit in new cars and eliminate ones that are no longer actively raced. Class A is mainly 427 Corvettes and 427 Cobras. Other Corvettes are in B with Ferraris and the hotter 911 Porsches. Class C is for TR Triumphs and some Lotus, Datsun and other Porsche models, while D includes everything from AC Bristols through Fiat Abarths to Yenko Stingers.

Alfa Romeos are strong in Class E, with Elvas, MGBs and older Porsches. F fits in Triumph Spitfires, Datsuns and MGAs. But there are some earlier Spitfires in Class G, along with Healey Sprites and MG Midgets. The smallest category, Class H, is for the early Sprites, Fiat 850 Spiders, Morgan 4/4s and the 1100cc version of the Opel GT. All these are only samples; almost 200 cars are listed by name in the classifications, including some you've probably never heard of, such as the WSM, Sabra, Fairthorpe, Turner, GSM and Speedwell. You can't say they're trying to keep anybody out.

The closest and frequently the finest road racing for these production sports cars can be seen in the series of National races. At least six weekends of races and as many as twelve are run in each of the seven geographical divisions to determine the top drivers in twenty-one classes of cars. Competititon in these Nationals is spirited, with hundreds of amateur drivers competing in sixty-odd events at scores of sites throughout the country. The best qualify for the American Road Race of Champions in November, with the winners there becoming the National Champions in each class.

This ARRC, as it's known, is a relatively recent invention—like many of the best things about road racing. Early in 1963 the idea arose almost simultaneously among the staff members of *Sports Car Graphic*, then headed by John Christy, and some SCCA members in the Eastern Tennessee Region, that it would be great to find a way to bring together the top class winners from each division to compete with each other head-to-head. Both suggested this to the SCCA headquarters, with the result that the first ARRC was scheduled at Riverside, California, for November 1964. An early objection was that those racers for whom Riverside was the "home circuit" would enjoy an unfair advantage, but this has been found to be less significant than differences in cars and drivers. Since '64 the race has alternated between Riverside and Daytona, Florida, to give each coast a crack at it. A central location, such as the new Dallas track, may be used in the future.

ARRC invitations go to the six top finishers in all the racing classes in each SCCA division. Accepted ARRC entries are limited to the top three submitting an entry from each class. Thus no more and usually no less than three from each class uphold a division's honor against the six other divisions' counterparts, a total of twenty-one cars in each race.

These twenty-one are already winners, frequently having gained the coveted ARRC spot after an emotionally charged session of racing that has consumed wife, family and friends in the single-minded pursuit. At the stages on the way, the National races where points must be won, 4000 drivers compete with the objective of "ARRC at Thanksgiving." Four hundred of the 4000 make it. Neither the National races nor the ARRC has race track purses, only trophies as direct rewards for finishing.

The ARRC is often called the "Olympics of sports car racing" which is at least twice a misnomer, but convenient. Eligibility for the ARRC runoffs is limited to SCCA's national championship program within the United States, and nine of the twenty-one classes are for small sedans and single-seaters having nothing to do with sports cars.

Easily as characteristic of the ARRC as of the Olympics is the heavy commercialization. Few sports are as commercially oriented as auto racing and there is little distinction between SCCA's club racing today and so-called professional racing in SCCA or any other sanctioning organization. SCCA has long ceased distinguishing between amateur and professional drivers and has successfully abandoned the term "amateur" in favor of "club" in recent years. Few race drivers anywhere in the world are so thoroughly professional as some of the top contenders in the ARRC. For these reasons—interest of car makers and accessory companies in victories to advertise—few race events anywhere attract greater total cash rewards. SCCA estimates that each recent ARRC involved more than $65,000 in checks made out to participating drivers.

Such a large and costly affair wouldn't be possible without the

Former national champion Bob Tullius accepts the checkered flag and congratulations after outrunning four C-Production Porsches in his Triumph TR6 at a recent SCCA national championship sports car race.

sponsorship first obtained by SCCA in 1967. Two firms without direct automotive interest have co-sponsored the event with financial and publicity support. They are Nine Flags International, a division of Gillette, marketing a line of men's grooming products, and Newspaper Enterprise Association, a syndicated newspaper feature service.

A $40,000 SCCA travel fund collected by assessment throughout the year is distributed to invited drivers to cut their costs, in proportion to their travel distance. In addition, such companies as Datsun, Union Oil, Volkswagen, British Leyland, Valvoline, Gulf, Champion Spark Plug, Ford and American Motors have award schedules that pay directly for high finishes in the ARRC. Considerably weightier financial support is given throughout the year by some car makers to official and semi-official drivers and teams seeking dominance in the club racing program. The members of these teams, including the drivers, are in fact employees of business operations solely devoted to racing, giving them a professional classification as indisputable as that of any race drivers in the world.

Also, scores of sponsors ranging from Owens-Corning Fiberglas to the corner garage help place cars and teams on the starting grids by absorbing all or part of the considerable expense of racing an automobile. All of this is for the publicity convictions held by companies on the one side and for very compelling tax considerations on the part of the individual drivers.

As a spectacle the ARRC is a dazzling kaleidoscope of race cars, tow cars and trailers for 2500 drivers and crew members; tents, trucks and banners of participating companies; an almost endless series of free parties for the drivers (to go with their free motel rooms), and a swarm of celebrities, journalists and publicists.

But car-to-car and driver-to-driver competition is the pure, hard flame at the core of the ARRC. Drivers may be competing wheel-to-wheel against those whom they have battled all season. Or one may find himself dueling a never-met driver from another division. Competition between car makes, whether or not heavy sponsorship is involved, attracts avid loyalties. Finally, the ARRC pits the various SCCA divisions against each other, unofficially, to see which one is best by winning the most SCCA championships.

If you count success by the number of championships collected, the Southern Pacific division is well in the lead with a total of 41 recorded in 1964 through 1969. Drivers from the Northeast rank next with 28 championships, just ahead of the 27 won by representatives of the Northern Pacific division. From the Central division have come 23 champions, and less than ten each from the remaining three divisions.

But divisions don't race each other at Daytona, or Riverside, or Dallas. Men and women do, probing their own abilities as they can in no other sport, riding in the wheeltracks of some of the world's greatest drivers. And all that begins in a one-car garage, and a station wagon with a trailer hitch, with printed "PADDOCK" stickers on the windshield.

Bruce McLaren consults with crew member during a pit stop at the 1967 Sebring 12 hours of endurance. McLaren and Mario Andretti went on to win in the Ford Mark IV.

2 THE LONG-DISTANCE CLASSICS

Time was when we only saw the great European factory teams once a year in this country. Ferrari, Jaguar, Porsche, Maserati and Aston Martin had only one chance to bring Hawthorn, Moss, Fangio, Collins, Trintignant, Ascari and Taruffi to North America to race their cars, and we had one chance, just this one, to see these great men and cars in action. Incredibly, we had to go to an airport in Florida near a town with no other visible reason for existence to take advantage of this opportunity.

Today the machines and men from Italy, France, Germany, Britain and New Zealand are here throughout the year, shuttling back and forth on the big jets. Mortals now, not heroes, we can watch them at Mosport, Watkins Glen and Riverside. In Florida at

Daytona there's a twenty-four-hour race as well as the twelve-hour event that started it all, at Sebring. Now there's also a six-hour endurance race at Watkins Glen, New York.

Six hours is a long time to race. Twenty-four hours is, for many men and cars, entirely too long: "Six, twelve, twenty-four—What the hell do we do it for?" There's a reason. It concerns mainly the egos of men and the reputations of companies. There is little in it that is fun, if by fun in motor racing we understand the mind-stretching exhilaration of controlling a Grand Prix car at the ultimate brink of speed, or the pleasure that comes from tucking away the five-figure victory check from a Can-Am race.

Modern long-distance sports car racing traces its origins to two great classics: France's Le Mans race and Italy's Targa Florio. Le Mans in particular was a titan among car competitions since it was first established in the early Twenties as a day-long event catering to cars that are of the road going type. The Bentley victories there spread the race's fame in the English-speaking world, as did the Jaguar wins in the Fifties. When America's Briggs Cunningham started building his own sports cars in 1951, he did so with the main objective of winning the Le Mans race.

A Cunningham car never won Le Mans, but one did win at Sebring in 1953, the first season an official Championship for car makers was put into effect by the FIA. It's this Championship, known today as the International Championship for Makes, backed up by the International Cup for Grand Touring Cars, that knits together the ten or eleven events longer than six hours or 1000 kilometers that are run each year, from February through August, for sports, prototype and GT cars. Three of these races are run in America, and the first one, Sebring, was by its own admission an imitation of Le Mans.

To Briggs Cunningham and many others involved with the birth of the Sebring race in 1950, Florida was home country, home for one part of the year, at least. To them, wintering at West Palm Beach, Sebring didn't seem as remote as it did to the rest of the country and the world. Cunningham loaned the money to pay the insurance premium for the first event, entered Phil Walters in a

Cadillac Healey, and drove an Aston Martin himself. George Huntoon of Palm Beach was a tower of strength in that first six-hour race, on the last day of 1950, briefing the drivers before the start, and taking time to explain what was happening to Florida's Governor Warren and Senator Moore, whose support for a more elaborate event in the future was being solicited.

"Discovery" of Sebring as a possible track site was aided by Miles and Sam Collier, the great road racing enthusiasts whose family had owned a substantial chunk of Florida's Collier county. An aerial survey in Sam's Beech Bonanza showed the maze of runways and service roads the old B17 training base offered. Watching from the ground was Colonel Claude D. Richardson, Jr., who was in the aircraft parts business at the base and active in Sebring's affairs. He was able to interest the town firemen in putting on the first races there; without their help it wouldn't have been possible.

Also involved in the planning, especially in the decision to pattern the race after Le Mans and highlight the Index of Performance award, was Alexander Edward Ulmann. The ebullient Alec and his wife Mary had been behind the scenes at the first Watkins Glen race in 1948, and Alec's business involvement with aviation brought him into the Sebring scene. Since then, with the help of Chet Flynn and Tim Howkins and the year-round services of Reggie Smith as race secretary, the Ulmanns have made the race what it is—or isn't—today, behind the wheeled-alligator emblem of the Automobile Racing Club of Florida.

Fred Wacker and Frank Burrell went the farthest in that first race in their Cad-Allard with Hydra-Matic drive, but were only eighth on Index. The stove-stock Crosley that took first wasn't even entered until just before the race, when Tommy Cole tried it and found it was very quick as long as you slid the corners and didn't try to shift it. Fritz Koster and Bob Deshon did just that, making only one fuel stop, to take the win.

The track was different then, only 3½ miles long. The pits were on the opposite side of the front straight, with a jog to the left bringing the cars closer to them. Just past the pits the track turned left onto the service roads, about where today's concessions area ends.

The cars came onto the runway again where the Webster Corners used to be. The two long straights were just as they are today: completely dull and death on brakes.

In '52 the race obtained the March placing on the calendar that it still has. Through the AAA the Ulmanns gained international recognition for the event in 1953, though we're assured by the Automobile Competition Committee of the United States (ACCUS) (contrary to what Alec and most contemporary reports said) that the race didn't actually count toward Manufacturer's Championship points until 1954. That was the year Briton Stirling Moss and American Bill Lloyd drove an 87ci Italian OSCA to an overall win, finishing with no brakes at all. The truth of this was demonstrated to a disbelieving Laurence Pomeroy by Moss, who easily pushed the OSCA down the track in spite of the best the rotund "Pom" could do with the brake pedal.

Joe Lane's official timers and scorers had their greatest challenge in 1955 when two teams, Carroll Shelby/Phil Hill (Ferrari) and Mike Hawthorn/Phil Walters (Jaguar), came to the winner's circle to collect the cup. At a review several weeks later Joe's conclusion that the Jaguar had won was upheld. That was one of the last official

AAA acts in connection with Sebring, which found itself without a sanction to stand on when that body pulled out of racing in mid-'55. Eventually a co-existence with the SCCA was evolved that still serves well.

In those days there was no requirement that a certain number of cars be produced to qualify one to race; only that the maker was validated by his national automobile club as a bona fide automobile manufacturer. If he was so qualified he could enter "prototypes" of cars he said he might put into production sometime in the future. The sports/racing cars built to suit such rules were out-and-out racing machines with fenders and headlights and spare tires, usually roadsters, like the light, tough 3.5-liter four-cylinder Ferrari that Juan Fangio and Eugenio Castellotti drove to victory at Sebring in 1956.

Juan Manuel Fangio, the Argentine who is among the greatest road racers the world has ever seen, switched from Ferrari to Maserati in 1957 and won at Sebring again. He did it with the most formidable sports/racer of that era, the V8 450/S Maserati, against top Ferrari and Jaguar opposition. Frenchman Jean Behra was his co-driver. An utter failure gathered most of the press attention:

In a truly spectacular performance against the world's finest cars and drivers at a recent Sebring endurance trial, three MGAs, driven by American amateur drivers, captured the coveted International 12-hour Grand Prix of Endurance Team Trophy.

The 1965 Sebring 12-hour race was a wet one. A sudden deluge flooded the course, giving the smaller-displacement cars an advantage. Here a Ferrari goes cautiously down the straight, while a Sprite may be just behind, readying to pass at a higher speed.

Chevrolet's factory-built Corvette SS, a completely special car developed by Zora Arkus-Duntov and driven—for only twenty-three laps—by John Fitch and Piero Taruffi.

Endurance racing changed shape in 1958 when its governing authority, the FIA in Paris, decided the cars were getting too fast and clamped down a maximum engine size of 3000cc or 183ci for those cars that would qualify for the Championship. Under the new rules Aston Martins were quick, as Stirling Moss showed with the fastest lap at Sebring, but victory went to the V12 Ferrari of Phil Hill and Peter Collins.

With one interruption, a Porsche win in 1960 when the factory cars were kept home by a fuel contract dispute, Ferrari had a hammerlock on America's only endurance race from 1958 through 1964. A rear-engined Ferrari first raced there in 1961, but front-engined models came home first in '61 and '62. Then rear-engined V12 models took over the victories through 1964. In 1962 the Championship in these events had been switched from sports/racers to Grand Touring cars. This didn't make any difference to Enzo Ferrari because his cars monotonously won this category too at Sebring, until 1964, when Carroll Shelby's home-brewed Cobra scored a GT win in the hands of Bob Holbert and Dave MacDonald.

With the war between Ford and Ferrari turning from cold to hot, endurance racing Sebring-style was gathering momentum fast. But now the circus had two rings, both in Florida, with acts going on just a month apart. There was now another long-distance race, at

Jim Hall's revolutionary Chaparral 2F caused quite a stir at the 1967 Daytona 24-hour race, appearing in GT coupe fashion for the first time, driven by Hall and Mike Spence.

Ferrari finished one, two, three at the 1967 Daytona
Continental, led by Lorenzo Bandini and Chris Amon.

the Daytona International Speedway, using a 3.81-mile combination
of the bankings and the infield road course. In 1966, for the first
time, it counted for Championship points.

Bill France, NASCAR president and proprietor of the pioneering
Daytona track, had been gradually grooming his "Continental" for
Championship status. He did so with a shrewd assessment of the
interests of the men in Europe who govern international racing. The
first Continental was a three-hour affair in 1962, historic for its victory by Dan Gurney in a Lotus 19. Dan's car crossed the finish line,
as the rules required, "under its own power"—provided by the
starter motor, not the engine!

In 1963 the evergreen Pedro Rodriguez from Mexico was the
winner of the three-hour Continental, in a Ferrari. The following
year Pedro teamed up with Phil Hill to drive an LM-bodied Ferrari
GTO in a Continental that had been expanded to 2000 kilometers

in length, about 1240 miles. They won the race in a little more than 12 hours and 40 minutes, giving Daytona a longer event than Sebring and marking the first time the banked track had been used for racing at night.

Still at 2000 kilometers and still not counting for points, the 1965 Continental was attended by a single factory 330 P2 Ferrari roadster entered privately by Luigi Chinetti's New York-based North American Racing Team. Surtees and Rodriguez had tire troubles with it which handed the race to the rejuvenated GT40 Fords entered by Carroll Shelby's stable. Ken Miles and Lloyd Ruby handled the winner. Then the Fords went to Sebring to contest one of the oddest events in that track's history. Alec Ulmann wangled FIA permission to let sports/racing cars enter, clearing the way for a surprise win by Jim Hall and Hap Sharp in a plastic, automatic-transmission Chaparral. A GT40 and Cobra Coupe fought through torrential rains to win the prototype and GT classes respectively.

In '66 and '67, of course, we had the peak years of the Ford-Ferrari battle, with Chevy-supported Chaparral a fast but erratic interloper. The focal point of their efforts was Le Mans, which still offered the peak prestige of the endurance racing world. The two American events were little more than tuneups for these titans. In 1966 Daytona gathered more than token importance when Bill France extended it to a full twenty-four hours and had it listed, for the first time, as a Championship event.

With an armada of five Mark II coupes powered by 427ci wedge engines, Ford faced only private Ferraris and a single Chaparral at Daytona. It collected a one-two-three victory with Ken Miles and Lloyd Ruby in the winning car. Driving an open-topped version of the Mark II, the same duo won at Sebring when Dan Gurney's leading Mark II coupe broke down on the last lap. The remaining Fords were sufficient to give Dearborn another one-two-three victory.

Ferrari had sent only a single factory 330 P3 to Sebring in 1966. It had been fast enough to contest for the lead but had retired with gearbox trouble. Following a policy of supporting alternate American events in successive years, Ferrari decided to mount an all-out offensive at Daytona in 1967. Late in '66 it brought a test car there

25

and the '67 team of three of the lovely P4 coupes was superbly prepared.

Ford, meanwhile, obliged Ferrari by fitting wrongly heat-treated shafts in the gearboxes of its six Mark IIs, causing them to break down with regularity through the whole twenty-four-hour race. Ferrari went home happy after a one-two-three finish of its own, led by Lorenzo Bandini and Chris Amon, while Ford went back to work to produce the Mark IV coupe that won at Sebring, driven by Bruce McLaren and Mario Andretti, after a rousing duel with the Chaparral 2F coupe handled by Mike Spence and Jim Hall. It was a clear victory of Ford over Chevy after a real *mano-a-mano* battle.

The ground rules of international endurance racing changed radically right after Ford's second Le Mans win in 1967. The FIA decided with startling suddenness that in 1968 entries should be limited to 183ci (3000cc) prototypes, 305ci (5000cc) "sports cars," built in lots of fifty per year, and GT cars without a limit on displacement but with a much higher production requirement. It was a complicated arrangement which (1) knocked factory Fords and Chaparrals out of endurance racing, (2) discouraged Ferrari for a full season and (3) effectively handicapped the remaining racers.

Something else new was added in 1968: America's third circuit as part of the International Championship for Makes. It came as something of a bombshell when the Watkins Glen organizers announced they'd stage a six-hour race in July, qualifying for points, and an even bigger surprise came in 1969 when the endurance race was made a curtain-raiser the day before a Can-Am race! But it worked, and the Glen Six Hours has become an important addition to the international calendar, even if one British writer did call it "an international club race."

That British veteran of endurance racing, John Wyer, was to startle the world in 1968 with the performance of his reworked GT40 Fords, collecting both the coveted Le Mans win and the Championship. But when the season started, in the first two American races it looked as though he'd embarked on a quest Don Quixote would have considered hopeless. Porsche won them both

John Fitch, at the wheel of a factory-built Chevrolet Corvette SS, starts alongside Jean Behra in the 1957 Sebring-winning Maserati.

with their 2200cc cars, Hans Herrmann and Jo Siffert having a hand in driving both winning coupes. Trans-Am cars figured strongly in both fields, a Mustang being fourth at Daytona and a Camaro third at Sebring.

The Porsches, not the Fords, had problems at Watkins Glen, new 183ci German models suffering from teething troubles. Wyer's Gulf-sponsored GT40s were one-two, followed by an unusual American car, the Howmet TX turbine-powered coupe. Porsche parked many of its mechanical problems in America and found them waiting when it returned in '69. Engines broke at Daytona and chassis at Sebring, leaving victory to the Chuck Parsons–Mark Donohue Lola Chevy in the first race and the Jackie Ickx–Jackie Oliver GT40 in

Ken Miles and Lloyd Ruby drove the open-cockpit Ford
Mark II to victory at the 1966 Sebring 12-hour race.

the second. Watkins Glen was another story, the Porsche 908 roadsters cruising to a one-two-three win.

Enzo Ferrari, who finds it hard to stay away from interesting racing, made a quiet comeback to the endurance classics in 1969 with
a 183ci V12 roadster that fell only one lap short of a victory at
Sebring. Both Porsche (with a half-year lead) and Ferrari equipped
their arsenals for the Seventies by building 12-cylinder 305ci
sports/racing cars, qualifying them at that engine size before the
FIA by building twenty-five identical cars. Their first field encounter
came at Daytona, where the Porsche's edge in field experience paid
off in victory for the 917, now being managed by the John Wyer
organization. The tables were turned at Sebring, where the Porsches
had front hub troubles, giving the win to a Ferrari 512.

Ferrari and Alfa Romeo from Italy, Matra and Alpine from
France, Porsche from Germany, Lola and Ford from Britain—

these have been the main characters in the long-playing drama that we're offered in the U.S. in our choice of six, twelve or twenty-four acts. The quality of endurance racing will change as the FIA's rules do, converging toward competition for 183ci prototypes only by 1972. This will make the endurance racers essentially Grand Prix cars with lights, fenders and engines that will run three to twelve times as long as they usually have to.

There's little glory in this kind of racing, where machines count the most and men are asked to meet assigned target speeds while not racing each other and not running off the road. There's exhaustion, sleeping in trailers behind the pits or, more likely, not sleeping at all. There's sheer hard work, juggling massive tires, sizzling hot brake pads, clumsy fuel cans and hoses, stopwatches and lap counters. There's uncertainty, irritation and despair.

But there is vast satisfaction in winning a race like Sebring or Daytona. Such a victory means you have outplanned, outthought, outprepared, outschemed, outpsyched, outdriven and sometimes outraced some of the best in the business. And after twenty-four hours —well, you know you've done a lot of auto racing.

Plymouth entered the Trans-Am series for the first time in 1970, with Dan Gurney and Swede Savage as pilots. Gurney soon backed out of the series as a driver; Swede continued, switching cars as they suited him. Here he leads Jones and Donohue in Gurney's Number 48.

3 SEDANS ON THE ROADS

Ever since the SCCA's Trans-American Championship made road racing for sedans one of the most colorful and successful forms of motor sport in America, everybody's been trying to take credit for doing it first. If the truth be known, everybody may deserve the honors, because sedan racing on road courses has been part of the American Scene since NASCAR stockers ran at Linden, New Jersey, in 1954 and the first "Little Le Mans" was off to a running start at Lime Rock in 1957.

Sedans and road courses didn't seem to mix at first. By its very name, and inclination as well, the Sports Car Club of America was anti-sedan for the most part. Occasionally a VW would appear in novice racing, but that's as far as it was allowed to go, unless the top were sliced off, as "Pup" Pupilidy did. NASCAR, however, had no hesitations about sedans; to Bill France's organization it was the road racing that presented the problem.

France brought his men and cars to the newest and best road course in the country, at Elkhart Lake, in August of 1956. A two-day program included a Saturday race for cars under 3500cc. It was a shoo-in for Paul Goldsmith driving a white Mark VII Jaguar. Placed fourth was Bill France, Jr., in a British Ford Zephyr. In the rain-delayed Sunday feature Mercurys prepared by Bill Stroppe placed one-two, Tim Flock in the lead. Over the 250 miles they survived early challenges by Buck Baker's Dodge and the Fords of Marvin Panch and Curtis Turner. With electric fans cooling finned brakes these massive sedans averaged 71.485 mph; sports/racers were doing about 80 mph over 100 less miles.

Stock cars of both USAC and NASCAR also enjoyed outings at Willow Springs and Paramount Ranch at that time. Entering the Sixties, Dan Gurney applied a little "reverse English" when he had Bill Thomas prepare a Chevy Impala to go to Britain, to contest the Jaguar dominance of road racing there. Dan was on the brink of cleaning up in British competitions when he encountered arbitrary problems with approval of his car that discouraged him.

In 1962 the USAC stock cars raced on roads only once in North America, at Mosport in Canada. The following season saw an explosion of road races for the big stockers, coming just as the Big Three were unwrapping some potent new racing engines. In '63 USAC and NASCAR staged road races at Riverside, Indianapolis Raceway Park, Bridgehampton, Meadowdale and Augusta. The next year the last two were dropped and replaced by Watkins Glen and Mid-America, and in '65 new tracks in the series were Greenwood Roadway and Mid-Ohio.

NASCAR Grand National stock cars last raced at Bridgehampton in 1966. In '67 Bill France's cars turned right only at Riverside, in the Motor Trend 500 that's become a classic early season event. Owned for so long by Dan Gurney, the Riverside race remained the only road race on NASCAR's calendar into 1970, when it was joined by another road event over 400 miles at the same track.

Swede Savage

Roger Penske

Mark Donohue

Parnelli Jones

Milt Minter

Sam Posey

USAC's stock car circuit has depended more on road events and is also better suited to them, now that the shorter-wheelbase "pony cars" are allowed to compete together with the "intermediates." At the twisty Sears Point course in California, where the two types first shared a starting grid early in '70, a Camaro was second behind a Road Runner and four of the sporty cars placed in the top ten finishers. Other USAC road events on the 1970 schedule included the new track at Dallas, Indianapolis Raceway Park, Summit Point, Pocono and Wentzville.

Big, loud and tough, the stock cars always put on a spectacular show on the road circuits. They take up a lot of track in the turns, often using the nearby real estate as well. The high-speed action in the pits is another bonus to the road racing fan who sees it otherwise only in Trans-Am racing. Three-speed transmissions and drum brakes handicapped the stockers in the Fifties, but now with discs, four speeds forward and limited-slip differentials, plus a lot more suspension know-how, they're more than able to handle any road going assignment.

In these days of twin-cam British Fords, BMW 2002s and Alfa Romeo GTA coupes it's hard to recall how little there was to work with, for racing, among the small foreign sedans back in the Fifties. Yet where there are cars there will be races, and so it was with the endurance events that catered at first to the imports only, and later to the new generation of compact American sedans.

The first "Little Le Mans," a ten-hour race for imports under 1600cc, was staged at Lime Rock, Connecticut, in October 1957. Through 1962, when it was last held, this developed into a most enjoyable and relaxed kind of competition—though it was taken seriously enough by the potential winners and the factory-backed teams that took part.

Both the first and last Little Le Mans races were won by Volvos. Nothing else eligible to race could come close to the toughness and durability at speed of the Volvo fastback sedans. The only competitors that had a chance were also from Sweden, the two-door SAAB sedans with their screaming, popping two-stroke engines. The picture changed momentarily in 1959 when the race was shortened to eight hours and GT cars of less than 1100cc and $4500 were admitted, allowing Roger Penske and Skip Callanan to win with an Abarth Fiat coupe—but only after the leading Volvo of perennial winners Art Riley and Bill Rutan retired.

Other tracks also staged interesting endurance racing for the smaller sedans. Continental Divide Raceways promoted the first "showdown" between the imports and the compacts, in which a well proven model—the AMC Rambler—ambled home first. The tight 1.7-mile track at Marlboro, Maryland, became the home of a grueling twelve-hour event. It was also dominated by Volvos until Ford started developing racing versions of its Cortina. In '63 Cortina GTs were first and second, an order repeated by Lotus Cortinas in 1964. Even though cars of up to 305ci were allowed in the six-hour running in 1965, an Alfa Romeo TI was the winner.

When Alec Ulmann decided to put on the first modern United States Grand Prix (see Chapter 8) at his Sebring, Florida, airport circuit in 1959, he realized he could use one or two curtain-raisers to enliven a potentially dull program. One, called a Compact Car Race, drew two Volvos, two Corvairs, three of the new Plymouth Valiants, three V8-engined Studebaker Larks driven by Curtis Turner, Fireball Roberts and Ralph Moody, and two Jaguar 3.4 sedans from the Briggs Cunningham stables handled by Walt Hansgen and Ed Crawford.

Chrysler's products battle it out at Laguna Seca, with Sam Posey's Dodge Challenger leading Swede Savage's Plymouth Barracuda into the turn.

This harmless-sounding Compact Car Race produced an epic battle over Sebring's full 5.2-mile circuit. At the end of the two-hour event the Hansgen Jaguar was in the lead, ahead of Turner's Lark and Crawford's Jaguar. Though the Grand Prix wasn't held at Sebring again, sedan races tailored more closely to imports became part of the prerace scene for the twelve-hour sports car endurance event. And that, indirectly, led to the creation of the Trans-Am Championship that's now one of the brightest jewels in the SCCA's professional crown.

The Trans-Am idea had its beginnings late in 1965 in a conversation between Reggie Smith, secretary of the Sebring races, and Jim Kaser, then the SCCA competition director. Smith wondered if there might be a way to link his curtain-raiser with other events, like that at Marlboro and an endurance race for sedans at Green Valley, Texas, to create a series that would benefit everyone mutually.

Kaser took the idea and ran with it. First he contacted car builders and importers, learning that they felt it was a great idea and would move to field or support teams in such a series. Then he got in touch with promoters, offering them a new kind of race with readily recognizable cars and a modest purse requirement, about $5000. Little did they know, when they accepted Kaser's proposition, that they'd be committed to purses five times as big by 1970.

Mid-America (Missouri), Bryar (New Hampshire), VIR (Virginia) and Riverside (California) joined the original three tracks to make the first Trans-Am in 1966 a seven-event series. It was an interesting year. A young up-and-coming Austrian named Jochen Rindt won the first Trans-Am race ever in an Alfa GTA, appropriately enough at Sebring. The Dodge Dart of Bob Tullius was second, and later in the year was first to cross the line when the Marlboro event was stretched out to twelve hours again. With his co-driver, Tony Adamowicz, who became Continental Champion in 1969, Tullius led a sweep of the first four places for Chrysler Corporation products.

Only at the twisty Bryar track, with Alan Moffat driving, did an under-2000cc car win overall again in 1966, a Ford Lotus Cortina. Otherwise it was a season for big Fords, the Mustang coupes with

All American Racers went first class all the way in 1970 with a van housing their two Plymouth Barracudas.

289ci engines winning the rest of the races and collecting the Championship, which was established for makes of cars, not for drivers. Alfa Romeo came out on top in the under-2000cc category, in those simpler days before somebody in Stuttgart figured out how to get the FIA to accept the Porsche 911 as a "sedan."

Technically the Trans-Am has been open to Group 1 and Group 2 Touring Cars, as defined in Appendix J of the Sporting Code of the FIA. In addition, a maximum wheelbase of 116 inches and maximum displacement of 305ci were imposed. This was just right, of course, for the new generation of long-hooded, short-decked sporty cars from Detroit. There manufacturers usually concerned only with AMA specification forms soon learned the tricks of the trade of FIA homologation papers.

As Chrysler had the year before, the Ford Motor Company in 1967 decided to allow two of its divisions to tear each other apart in Trans-Am racing, to the detriment of their corporate domination of the Championship. It worked better for Ford than it had for Chrysler, with Mustang finally edging Cougar for top rank in Trans-Am by a scant two points. A complete newcomer, Chevrolet, was in third place, surprisingly close to the other two.

There'd been eighteen requests for Trans-Am race dates in 1967, which Jim Kaser and company trimmed back to a tidier twelve.

Jim Hall entered his Chaparral Camaros in 1970, winning only one race, Watkins Glen, with Vic Elford at the wheel.

This time Daytona was the lead-off race, a 300-miler won by Bob Tullius and his trusty Dodge. But in later races the Dart was no match for the Shelby Mustangs of Jerry Titus and the Bud Moore Cougars of Dan Gurney, Parnelli Jones, Peter Revson and Ed Leslie. The last two events at Las Vegas and Kent brought a new name to the winner's circle: Mark Donohue/Chevrolet Camaro, entered by a Chevrolet dealer in Philadelphia, Pennsylvania, named Roger Penske.

Penske, a hard-driving young man who was an excellent road racing driver in Porsches, Maseratis, his own Cooper-based Zerex Special and in Chaparrals, gave up driving for team managing and, since 1965, the operation of a Chevrolet dealership. In 1966 Penske was entering a Corvette in the Florida long-distance races and tapped a driver-engineer his age, Mark Donohue, in mid-season to handle his Lola Type 70 in Group 7 events. At Mosport later that year Donohue won for Penske and his sponsor, the Sun Oil Company, the third-ever Can-Am race.

Chevrolet introduced its sporty Camaro in 1966 and, for the '67 model year, released cautiously a 5-liter version called the Z-28 which was eligible for Trans-Am racing. It was eligible but not yet suitable, as Penske and Donohue found when they started to prepare one for the 1967 season. Its excellent engine gave it fine performance but the chasiss was a riddle that took an entire season to decipher. After considering Jack Brabham as a chassis consultant,

Chevy decided to trust its brash Philadelphia dealer with the race development of the Camaro, setting a pattern of active engineering help and generosity with pieces—but *not* with actual money—that holds true to this day.

In 1967, as Mark Donohue said, "We raced it until it broke, then took the pieces to Chevrolet. They designed new ones and we put them in and ran it until something else broke." For 1968 Chevy fixed more pieces and made a new two-carburetor manifold that worked well, outstandingly so, bringing the Trans-Am Championship to Chevrolet with ten wins in thirteen events. For 1969 there was to have been another "goodie" from the Chevy engineers, aluminum cylinder heads with revised valves and porting, but these fell behind schedule and were never ready in time to be homologated, even by Chevy's experts in the art of writing recognition forms.

Roger Penske Racing fields an immaculate racing car. Others have equaled but not surpassed the precise, sanitary, professional presence of a product from the Penske shops. They are also smart. Penske and Donohue like to refer to their "innovations," which may be defined as exceedingly ingenious yet letter-perfect ways of interpreting the deliberately restrictive Trans-Am rules. The cold Pennsylvania winters are spent constructively by this team, thinking up creative new ways of going faster while probing deeply to find the absolute limits of the regulations.

> Sam Posey's Autodynamics Dodge Challenger leads Parnelli Jones' Mustang and Mark Donohue's Javelin at Elkhart Lake's Road America in 1970. Posey led the race for a while but lost it to Donohue.

Mark Donohue and Parnelli Jones were the best two competitors in Trans-Am racing, consistently neck and neck.

Penske's operation is also disarmingly small. There are no phalanxes of executive experts, no feuds and factions among members of the same family. Instead there is enthusiasm, a tight, deliberately selfish team spirit. Instead there is perspiration, with up to 1500 man-hours devoted to the preparation of each car and total teardowns between races. Instead there is youth. Much of Penske's crew is recruited from college students, free for the summer

In 1969, facing formidable Mustang competition, the Penske strategy was to go no more than fast enough. Mark Donohue explains: "Trans-Am racing isn't flat-racing. The idea is to go the whole distance and have a car underneath you at the end of the race. We wait until the first pit stop, hanging back and not straining the car, and then decide how fast we have to go."

Donohue did not need to add that at that point, after the first pit stop, he was almost certain to be in the lead. Thanks to intensive drilling by the crew and the design of innovative ice-cooled refueling equipment by Sunoco's Jerry Kroninger, plus push-to-open fuel filler doors that were new to the cars in 1969, the Penske team was able to get its fuel stops down to such incredible minimums as 3.3 (yes, 3.3) seconds. During a typical event the Camaros would have fuel stops averaging five to six seconds while those of the Fords were more than twice as long at twelve to fourteen seconds.

Late in the 1969 season the Fords were doing as well but by then it was, indeed, too late. At Sears Point, California, in the next-to-last race, Donohue locked up the Championship for Chevrolet with an exciting victory over a fast-closing Parnelli Jones.

Mustangs had taken the field in force in '69. Two were entered by the Carroll Shelby team that had carried the burden in 1968. Tires were Goodyear, drivers were Peter Revson, Horst Kwech and, when available, Dan Gurney. Two other cars went to Walter "Bud" Moore, the veteran of NASCAR stock car racing who prepared the Mercury Cougar team in 1967, keeping one of the cars for NASCAR's similar Grand Touring Division in '68. Moore's red and black cars ran on Firestones and were driven by George Follmer and Parnelli Jones—Ford's star talent.

This seemingly invincible juggernaut showed its muscle by winning the first two races at Michigan International Speedway and Lime Rock Park, the first with Parnelli Jones in a Moore car and the second with Sam Posey, a talented stand-in for Peter Revson, in a Shelby car. From this point, it seemed, the Fords could only continue to get better. But there were problems, in the axle and tire departments, that lost them the hardest-fought Championship in Trans-Am history.

With more factory teams and more open regulations, Trans-Am racing was tougher in 1970 than in '69—and it will be tougher still in the future. As the one team that was carried over almost without change, except for improvement, the Moore/Mustang/Jones/Firestone combination is a hard one to beat. Helped by greater freedom in rear suspension design and bore/stroke combinations allowed by the rules, but handicapped by the 1970 requirement for a single carburetor, the Javelins now fielded by the Penske team are reversing their losing form of their first two seasons.

Camaros from Chaparral and Owens-Corning, Firebirds from the Jerry Titus stable, Barracudas from Dan Gurney's AAR and Dodge Challengers from Autodynamics, driven by Sam Posey—strong cars with strong teams behind them make the Trans-Am the vital series that it's become in only four seasons. Road racing for sedans has come a long way from the Little Le Mans at Lime Rock.

41

Dan Gurney (48) took McLaren's place after his death and won his second consecutive Can-Am at St. Jovite for the team.

4 THE BIG BOOMERS

Racing on the roads has taken many forms over the years in America. Today we have sedans, production sports cars, formula cars, Grand Prix cars, sports/racing coupes and Indy cars tearing up road courses from one coast to the other. Significantly, though the richest and most respected road racing series in America is the one that best expresses the kind of competition we've enjoyed most and featured most prominently since we revived racing on roads at Watkins Glen in 1948: the booming big sports/racing cars.

The Sports Car Club of America was, after all, founded for the benefit of sports cars and their owners. After seven men met on the evening of February 26, 1944, they resolved that the purpose of the SCCA should be "to further the preservation of sports cars,

Jim Hall

Denis Hulme

Chuck Parsons

Bruce McLaren

to act an an authentic source of information thereupon and to provide events for these cars and their owners." There's no mention of single-seater racers, which for years were lumped by the SCCA into the "Unlimited" class. Sports cars reigned supreme.

From these beginnings grew the Canadian-American Challenge Cup series, with awards in 1970 totaling $875,000 in eleven races. When the Can-Am events began to take shape in 1965 and 1966, they were for sports/racing cars as defined in Group 7 of Appendix J of the FIA's International Sporting Code. There was some racing for such cars in Europe, too, in those days, and there's some in Japan today, but otherwise the Can-Am sports/racers have become a distinctly American phenomenon.

Phenomenal is the word for these cars, unfettered in design except for the most agreeable of rules, as powerful and light as their designers can make them and as men dare drive them. They are, in fact, the fastest road racing cars in the world, fastest in the sense of getting around a road course as quickly as possible. They've

Lothar Motschenbacher

Peter Revson

proved it several times, with faster lap speeds at tracks like Canada's Mosport where the Formula 1 Grand Prix cars also run. So far they haven't been matched, car for car, with the Indy machines set up for road racing, but the Can-Am two-seaters are likely to be quicker than these too. In fact it would be spectacular to see what one of the best Can-Am racers would do at Indy! Jim Hall didn't do badly when he tried a Chaparral there, and that was an old 2B model, several years back. The progress has been sensational since.

Nobody really knows how fast these cars will go. For all the tracks in the U.S. and Canada they're geared down, for maximum acceleration instead of top speed. Even so, at Riverside they're now touching 200 on the back straight. Considering that the Le Mans Mark IV Fords could do 220 mph with 100 less horsepower and a higher roof line, a top Can-Am car might be able to go 250 (!) with the right gearing.

One thing is certain: In spite of the fact that the Can-Am Championship is awarded to drivers, it's equipment that gets the job done in these events. Even the best drivers admit that there are some places on some tracks, like the downhill right-hander at Bridgehampton, where the cars are just *too* fast. As Dan Gurney found out in 1968, you can try to beat the more powerful cars with lightness and smartness, but it's very nearly impossible.

Can-Am equipment has evolved toward a blend of American and European design techniques. The engines are mainly American, with European power-producing ideas. Chassis are mainly European, with American aerodynamic ideas and tire concepts. Some competitors are all-American, some all-European, some all-Japanese. This evolution toward variety, the result of twenty years of development of unlimited sports/racing cars in the U.S., appropriately reflects the many different kinds of cars that have won the races for the big modifieds since the SCCA first got serious about road racing.

John Fitch used an American car, the Chrysler-engined C2 Cunningham, to win the first SCCA National Championship in 1951. While Cunningham concentrated on Le Mans, next year, Texan Sherwood Johnston piled up points with his light cycle-

Mark Donohue made "one show" in the 1969 Can-Am series, in the Penske Sunoco Lola at Mid-Ohio, then shelved the Can-Am project.

fendered Jaguar special. In '55 Johnston (who returned to competition in Formula A in 1969) won many SCCA Nationals with a Cunningham-owned D-Type Jaguar, a tradition that was carried on by Walt Hansgen in 1956 and '57 and in the following two years in Jaguar-powered British Listers.

Meanwhile 4.5-liter Ferraris enjoyed a period of dominance, 1953 with Bill Spear and 1954 with Jim Kimberly. Those were the years when the SCCA had a good thing going with General Curtis LeMay and the Strategic Air Command, giving them the use of SAC bases for road races, until Congress decided that wasn't such a good idea. Apart from Phil Hill's West Coast successes, including a class championship in 1955, Ferrari hasn't made much of an impression since among American sports/racers. The sheer torque of the big V8s from Detroit has been too much for the high-speed V12s.

A new era of bigger and better engines had opened in 1949,

In 1969 Jim Hall developed another revolutionary Chaparral, the 2H.

when Cadillac and Oldsmobile introduced their trend-setting over-head-valve V8 engines, with high compression, short strokes and big bores, and five main bearings. These engines were very responsive to tuning and reasonably light, at around 750 pounds, in relation to their displacement.

The same power race that was sparked by these new engines in the American automotive industry had a similar effect in American sports car racing. Prime beneficiary of this output explosion was Sydney Allard, who had coincidentally developed a chassis which was ideal for these big new V8s. In August 1949, the Allard Motor Company introduced the De Dion-axle, coil-suspended J2 competition model, a machine of questionable high-speed stability but uncanny ability to put power on the road. Briggs Cunningham, with Tom Cole, obtained one of the first J2s, and by January of 1950 had installed a stock 160 horsepower Cadillac engine. In June 1950, the Cadillac-Allard came of age, when Tom Cole won overall with one at Bridgehampton. Five Cad-Allards were entered at Watkins Glen in September, where they filled first and third places.

Also notable for outright wins, against top-flight opposition in imported machinery, were the ugly but effective Buick-powered specials of Californian Max Balchowsky. Max's Buick know-how was applied to Eric Hauser's Morgensen Special in 1957, the looks of which may be judged by the fact that its rear fenders, its only compound-curved parts, came from a 1949 Chevrolet truck. The car became known as "Old Yaller," and in 1959 Balchowsky continued the tradition with Old Yaller II, slightly less ugly, boasting independent front suspension, and just as successful, with a 400ci Buick for power.

When Lance Reventlow gathered a great team in Los Angeles to build the Scarab sports/racing cars, they selected the light, high-revving Chevrolet engine and transmission as a nucleus. Work began on the first Scarab in September 1957, six months before its shakedown runs. First 305 and later 340ci, the engines used Hilborn fuel injection and special big valves. They provided 375 bhp at 6000 rpm with 370 pound feet of torque at 4500, and offered power from 3000 to 7000 rpm. Later owners made further changes on the engines, in one case increasing the displacement to 350ci. These cars dominated U.S. competition in 1958, driven by Reventlow and Chuck Daigh, and were still capable of overall wins in 1963, handled by Augie Pabst and Harry Heuer.

Though the rear-engined configuration was to become dominant in competition car design in the Sixties, some builders pressed ahead with projects using the potent Chevrolet engine in front. One of the best of the breed was Jim Hall's first Chaparral, which took shape in 1961 in the shop of Dick Troutman and Tom Barnes, veterans of the Scarab project. Made extremely light, with modern British disc brakes and fully independent suspension, the first Chaparrals scored numerous wins in SCCA racing and were entered unsuccessfully at Sebring in 1963.

The last really successful front-engined car in top-line American sports car racing was the original Type 61 "Birdcage" Maserati, which first arrived in the U.S. in quantity in 1960. Driven by Walt

Hansgen, Gaston Andrey, Roger Penske, these light and stable cars ended the first "Chevrolet era" and made imports dominant once again. The Maserati in turn was demoted from the winners' lists in 1961, when Colin Chapman's first rear-engined sports car, the Lotus 19, became available. This car and its contemporary, the Cooper Monaco, were normally powered by the 150ci Coventry Climax FPF four-cylinder, which then delivered 240 bhp at 6800 rpm. Dan Gurney did wonders with a Lotus 19, and Coopers were successfully campaigned by Roger Penske and Hap Sharp.

Since late 1958 there had been a few money-paying road races in the U.S., spurred by USAC's establishment of a Road Racing Division that season. After 1962, however, USAC let its sports car racing series lapse. The Sports Car Club of America stepped resolutely into the professional picture in 1963 with the U.S. Road Racing Championship, a series for cash prizes and championship points for drivers and manufacturers. The USRRC embraced eight events in 1963, ten in 1964 and twelve in 1965, its high point before the Can-Am

Bruce McLaren (4) and Denis Hulme (5) were virtually unbeatable in the Can-Am series.

At the 1966 Bridgehampton Can-Am, Jim Hall unveiled his spectacular Chaparral 2E, with the huge rear wing, progenitor of all future racing "wings."

was established in 1966. The USRRC was continued until it was replaced by the Continental Championship for open-wheeled cars in 1969.

Late in 1963 the American sports/racing car began to evolve toward its present form. During that year, some aluminum blocks for Chevrolet V8s became available, in connection with Mickey Thompson's Indianapolis effort, and it wasn't long before these found their way into rear-engined sports cars. Such an engine weighed less than 500 pounds, yet could develop 450 bhp from 327ci, so it's not surprising that units of this type soon appeared in Coopers and Lotuses. One was installed in the rear-engined Scarab, which was used by A. J. Foyt in a devastating series of wins over the 1963-64 winter season.

From 1964 onward, owners of sports/racing cars began to benefit from the tremendous strides made by Firestone and Goodyear in the design of tires for Indianapolis. The new wider, more adhesive tires allowed much more latitude for experimentation and variation in weight distribution, specifically in getting as much weight as possible on the driving wheels without getting into handling difficulties. The net result was a new ability to use even larger, heavier and more powerful engines in the rear sports/racing cars. In fact in some cases it became a matter of the heavier, the better!

The outstanding example of this new school of thought was the Chaparral 2 of Jim Hall and Hap Sharp. Hall and Sharp used cast-iron Chevrolet V8 engines, both the normal 327ci size and a special 377ci version which, with Weber carburetion, was good for approximately 450 horsepower and extremely impressive torque. In combination with the reasonably low weight of its fiberglass structure, around 1300 pounds dry, this torque made it possible to use a hydraulic torque converter transmission in Chaparral 2.

Hall and Sharp laid waste to American road racing with their white cars in 1964 (with an assist from Roger Penske, before he retired from driving) and 1965. Hall won the USRRC in '64 and just missed it in 1965, the only year 2000cc cars had an equal chance to collect points. George Follmer was the '65 champ with his Porsche-powered Lotus. Late in 1965 Hall debuted his 2C, with the movable spoiler, and at Bridgehampton in 1966, in the second-ever Can-Am event, he and Phil Hill unveiled their spectacular 2E models, with the huge rear wing and rear-mounted radiators.

By winning three of the six events in 1966, balding Briton John Surtees became the first holder of the Johnson Wax Trophy that goes to the Can-Am Champion, plus the $48,100 that went with it. He used one of Eric Broadley's most versatile and successful designs, the Lola Type 70, with a Traco-prepared Chevrolet engine. Phil Hill won at Laguna Seca with the fabulous 2E Chaparral, which gave Bruce McLaren a lot to think about over the winter.

McLaren and his designer, Robin Herd, gave their new M6A McLaren for 1967 a monocoque frame recalling the Chaparral's in principle but resisted the temptation to go all the way to wings and rear radiators. With a well-developed car, a fine team and Denny Hulme as driver of a second orange McLaren, Bruce became Champion in '67 and the winner of a total of $62,300. Nineteen sixty-eight saw the new M8A McLaren win four of the six races, with a $93,060 Championship for Denny Hulme. Then in the extended 1969 Can-Am season Bruce took six of the eleven events in his winged M8B, collecting an aggregate of $160,950.

McLaren's machines, like most of the Can-Am cars, are powered by modified stock American V8 engines. There have been recent exceptions to V8 dominance. Ferrari had cars in 1967 for Ludovico Scarfiotti, Chris Amon and Jonathan Williams, in 1968 for Pedro Rodriguez and Amon, the latter a very fast special V12 racer with four overhead cams that came back to pose a strong challenge in 1969. Porsche also did well in '69 with a rebodied version of its 274ci flat-12 Type 917 endurance racing car.

The Ferraris and Porsches have to be taken seriously because they've stopped trying to prove that a small engine can beat a big one by revving faster, and have built big ones instead. Meanwhile the big ones are getting even bigger. Through 1969 most of the aluminum-block ZL-1 Chevrolets and "wedge" Fords were at 427ci. They were able to produce between 580 to 620 horsepower, revving

John Surtees (3) won three of the six events in the 1966 Can-Am series and became the first holder of the Johnson Wax Trophy. Here he leads Bruce McLaren at Mosport in 1966.

The Allard J2 (22) was introduced in 1949, turned into a Cadillac-Allard, and won races in the early fifties against such cars as the Ferrari America 4.1 here.

safely to 7000. The Seventies will see more of them nearer 488 cubic inches, larger than the biggest production car engine in the world, the 472ci Cadillac V8.

These very large engines could never have been used if Chevy and Ford hadn't moved, as they did, to cast the cylinder blocks in aluminum instead of iron. This saves just enough weight to allow the big V8s, also with aluminum heads, to be usable in the back of a light car. The aluminum block actually causes the engine to *lose* power, compared to an iron block, but they make up for that by slicing off the weight the power has to push.

In 1967, for the first time, McLaren annihilated the opposition in Can-Am racing with fuel injection. His were British Lucas injection systems, which gave his engines a little more power and a lot better, sharper response to the throttle. McLaren also used the vaporization of fuel in the manifold to cool the gasoline in the system, reducing the chance of vapor lock. This slick little trick had been borrowed from Grand Prix engines and was copied in 1968 by Traco and Bartz, two of the most important builders of Can-Am engines in the U.S. They also used Lucas injection, while Jim Hall uses a special Rochester injection on his Chaparral engines, which are prepared by Gary Knutson, McLaren's former engine builder.

Another important trend has been to what racers call "dry sump" engine oil systems. The sump or oil pan isn't actually dry, but neither is it asked to hold all the engine oil, as it probably does in your car. Instead there's an extra big oil pump whose only job is to suck the oil out of a shallow pan as it falls from the engine, and pump it to a separate oil tank. From there the oil pressure pump sends it to the bearings. The separate oil tank can hold much more oil than a conventional sump, allowing an engine to finish a race even if it's using a lot. A larger oil volume also stays cooler, helped by the separate oil radiators that are always used, and a properly designed tank can extract unwanted air from the oil.

Most Can-Am cars also carry a separate cooler for the oil in the transaxle, which can get pretty warm carrying high torques at high speeds. This is catered to by Britain's Mike Hewland, whose LG500 (four-speed) and LG600 (five-speed) transmissions are used in most of the top cars. The fastest don't always have more speeds; McLaren has used only four with the big Chevy because it has so much torque it doesn't need five speeds. And in the last few years Jim Hall's famous automatic box has become progressively less so, after starting out with only a hydraulic torque converter, like an old Buick Dynaflow. Then a second speed was added and finally a third one in the manually shifted box back of the converter. He had to do this after he lost the advantage in light weight the first Chaparral 2 had over its opposition.

In 1968, for the M8A, McLaren made a radical departure from convention by using the engine, with some tubular braces, as the rear part of the frame. The front of the engine was attached to the monocoque section and the rear part, where the transaxle was attached, carried the rear suspension. This helped Bruce keep the weight of his championship-winning car down to only 1450 pounds,

Briggs Cunningham produced his own road racer, the Cunningham C2, seen here at Elkhart Lake in 1952.

a little less than a Healey Sprite, an MG Midget or a Fiat 850 Roadster. How does it go with more than 600 horsepower? Pretty well, like zero to 100 in a little more than five seconds and certainly less than six.

Both Chaparral and McLaren have led the way in designing bodies for these cars that help hold the tires against the highway, replacing older styles that looked nice but tended to take off and fly. Certain common features are evident: a wide, scoop-like nose that's as close to the ground as possible; an upward flow of air out the back of the radiator; vents in the front fenders that keep air pressure from building up there, and a high, wide rear spoiler that deflects the air upward as it's departing. If the complete shape is a little like that of a wedge, or a doorstop, it's deliberate, made to shove its way under the air, producing forces that hold the car and its tires tightly against the road.

56

The Can-Am series enjoys international recognition by the FIA that permits star Grand Prix drivers like Brabham, Hulme and Amon to compete in the events, without restriction. This recognition carries with it the obligation to follow all FIA regulations that apply to the cars, which meant that when the high wings on Grand Prix cars were banned, they were also illegal on Can-Am machines, in spite of the SCCA's desire to keep them. (Series that don't have international status, like the Continental for Formula A cars, don't come under the ban so wings may still be worn.) New body design ideas give the strong downforce effects of wings without contravening the rules.

Such have been the growing pains of a great racing series. Some feared for its health and prosperity during the sudden expansion of 1969. With the continuation for a fifth year of the Johnson Wax sponsorship, the series is now solid at ten races from June through November.

Is this the way it will be? Is this as far as we'll go in the development of racing for the Group 7 cars we've bred in America? Judging by the past twenty years we won't stay satisfied with the way things are. The twenty just ahead should be spectacular.

The 1969 Lotus—from the famous Team Lotus racing stable—adopted the Indianapolis wedge shape, showing advanced thinking in terms of racing car aerodynamics.

5 FORMULAS FOR FUN

What does road racing need? What will make it and keep it widely understood and accepted among the American public at large? If a management consultant were called in to render a verdict, he'd certainly say that road racing has to be simplified. With all its classes, formulas and categories, he'd suggest, it's far too confusing. People, he'd say, will never be able to understand what's going on.

Those in charge of American road racing were well aware of this situation when representatives of new single-seater formulas came knocking on the door. First there were those fellows from Florida with their crazy idea about racing cars with stock Volkswagen engines! Then there was a demented bunch from England that thought there was some reason Americans should be interested in racing small cars with British Ford engines. Each eventually received its membership in Road Racing U.S.A., complicating the scene—and vastly enriching it at the same time.

Now that we have them, we can see that Formula Vee (Volkswagen) and Formula Ford (self-explanatory) are tremendously useful additions to our road racing repertoire. SCCA records show that the Vees have already done what their promoters promised: Helped train many of today's new star road racers. Vees and Fords both provide a relatively inexpensive way to get into serious racing. And though their spectator appeal has always been questioned, the International Motor Sports Association (IMSA) has used these two classes as the foundation of its professional road racing program.

Even at a fast track like Talladega, where these small, light cars should be completely unspectacular, they've put on heart-stopping shows. *National Speed Sport News* was impressed by a Formula Ford event: ". . . close, exciting competition . . . the first 11 cars Saturday finished within the same second . . . the foursome finished virtually under a blanket . . . event ended in a photo finish . . . few fans ever took their seats as tightly bunched packs of up to twenty cars jockeyed for an advantage . . . the drivers, enthusiastic as they were, frightened the veterans with their five-wide squadron flying on the banks."

Reluctant to give commercial plugs for free, the SCCA prefers the name "Formula F" for the Fords. IMSA has used the British term but may consider a completely different approach for the Fords, in time. There'll be no changing from "Formula Vee," however, for a kind of single-seater racer that's proved so popular that more than 2500 are now active in over twenty countries. The only switch has been to more of the same with the Super Vee class, created early in 1970 to allow the use of bigger 1600cc engines and more modifications.

And all this started with the conception that it would be possible to make a racing car out of—would you believe it—a Volkswagen, sometimes described as the lowest form of automotive life. In Germany VW-based race cars proliferated after the last war. They didn't have much else to work with. In America there were few

The Autodynamics Formula Vee was introduced in 1963.

VWs, let alone VW-based racers. The first one, spiritually the ancestor of the Formula Vee, has to be the car Kurt Hildebrand built with a belly tank body. It was the first car to retire from the first Sebring race on December 31, 1950. In only eight laps it made history.

Late in the Fifties, before there were dune buggies, or Formula 1 Porsches, or even Formula 2 Porsches to emulate, a man in Florida decided it might be fun to build a light little single-seat racer around stock VW parts. He had more than a casual interest, for he was the Southeastern U.S. Volkswagen distributor, Hubert Brundage of Brumos Motors.

Brundage contacted Enrico Nardi of Turin, Italy, in 1959 and asked him to make a prototype car. Nardi's working life, now concluded, encompassed an incredible variety of engine and car projects. Open-minded and resourceful, Nardi was the ideal man to present with such a commission.

Nardi kept the trailing arm front suspension and crossmember,

The essential ingredients of Formula Ford: the Cortina
GT family saloon, a Ginetta Formula Ford car (one of
twenty different marques taking part in formula races)
and the Cortina GT engine, the power behind it all.

complete with steering, and connected it by steel tubing to the rear
end assembly, with the engine positioned ahead of the rear wheels.
Trailing radius arms and coil springs replaced the original rear tor-

sion bar layout. Stock brakes and wheels were kept. Around the chassis went an aluminum body with a rounded, snub nose, a high back with a headrest and deeply cutaway sides. It had the look of stumpy harmlessness that clearly marked it as the first of the "angry overshoes."

Mr. Brundage, it seems, wasn't wild about Nardi's realization of his idea. It did make some racing appearances. At Daytona, in September 1960, Linley Colman took third with it behind a Cooper and a Porsche Super 90 in an SCCA Central Florida Region event. Then George M. Smith, a retired Air Force Colonel, entered the scene. Like some other enthusiasts, John Fitch among them, Smith couldn't see why auto racing wouldn't have room for a low-cost standardized car class, analogous to one-design sailboat racing. Smith saw the VW-based racer as road racing's equivalent of the Star class sailboat with which he'd completed enthusiastically.

"The cost of sailboat racing forbids it to many who would enjoy its thrills," wrote Colonel Smith in the SCCA magazine, *Sports Car,* "particularly in true racing craft. When the Star boat design first reached the market, it was known as the 'poor man's racing yacht.' The Formula Vee, by the same token, is designed to meet the needs of people who want to drive a real racing car, to enjoy the thrill of handling the wheel of a highly responsive vehicle, but cannot afford the upkeep of expensive, highly tuned thoroughbreds."

When his article appeared, in April 1963, Smith had already put his ideas in action. With another Floridian, Bill Duckworth, he built a modified fiberglass-bodied version of the Nardi in 1961, a sleeker machine with a lower back and higher sides. After tests at Sebring several more were made and sold. On July 1, 1962, Smith and Duckworth established Formcar Constructors, Inc., to promote the "Formcar" as a one-design racing machine.

Smith knew what the Formcar was supposed to be, but few others understood the idea then. At Savannah-Effingham Raceway in November 1962 four Formcars showed they had the legs of a field of F, G and H Production and H Modified cars. Over the 1962-63 winter Colonel Smith drafted a rigid set of rules governing car design and established the Formula Vee Racing Association to enforce them. With his Formcars mixing with production fields and trailing Formula Junior grids, Smith gained acceptance for a Southeast Division Championship.

In '63 builders could see the Vees were coming on strong. Late that year Florida's Gene Beach became Vee maker number two, creating the best body shape he could within the original rules, which included templates that actually fixed certain cross-section shapes, following, of course, the outline of the Formcar. Meanwhile, in far-away Massachusetts, a young General Electric Engineer had read the *Sports Car* article and concluded he'd build a Vee of his own. But Ray Caldwell couldn't believe that the SCCA, when it took the Vee formula under its wing in 1964, would adopt rules that would define the shape of a car so exactly. From the collision between Caldwell and Smith came a new set of rules that only generally described the areas the body has to cover, not the way it has to cover it.

In '64 Vees were honored with a National Championship classification by the SCCA, and the popularity of the idea was such that Vee racing went from nowhere to over seven hundred race entries that first year. From a single ad in *Sports Car Graphic* in October 1963, Ray Caldwell's new Autodynamics company received more than 1200 inquiries about Vee kits. Late that year Ray gave his prototype Vee a ten-minute test at Beverly Airport, Massachusetts, in the course of which the battery fell out and poured acid on the driver/builder.

Autodynamics Vee kits were first shipped in January 1964. They represented a new kind of Vee, built along modern racing car lines with a true space-type tubular frame and a longer, lower, slimmer body. Caldwell isn't so sure now that the aerodynamic advantage of the improved shape was so important but the enhanced appearance was certainly no handicap to sales. Neither was the performance in SCCA racing of Caldwell himself, who drove one of his products to the National Vee Championship that first year.

"We were the first with a professional approach to the class," Ray recalls. "I went out and tested the car and improved it and demonstrated it. We developed the car properly. But others have caught

The Lola T200 Formula Ford.

up to us now." In 1965 Autodynamics Vees took two of the SCCA divisional championships; Formcars took two more, and new names, Bobsy and Sardini, shared the last two. In the runoffs at Daytona a Beach came up the winner. Next year, at Riverside, a Zink car came in first, and has done so every year since. Ed Zink of Knoxville, Tennessee, owes his tremendous success to total concentration on the care and feeding of Vees.

Dedication like Zink's pays off, because Vee racing is a game of fractions of an inch. Rule interpretation is all-important. In a move similar to Caldwell's regarding the body, Gerry Mong of Bobsy tried to make a breakthrough to a monocoque frame for Vees. This time Caldwell was on the side of the *status quo*, and the rules continue to state specifically that "the frame/chassis shall be constructed of steel tubing of a maximum diameter or width of four inches . . ." Most Vees use tubing of about one-inch size.

Sharp engine tuning, while staying within the rules, is essential to success in Vee racing. So is the development of a super-smooth driving style. Vees have so little power that kinetic energy, once obtained, has to be hoarded greedily at every point around a race track. The correct line in a Vee is the one of least resistance, tracking corners rather than drifting them as might be done in a more powerful car. And after a few events the Vee driver gains respect for the hazards of exposed wheels in close-fought competition, respect that will serve him well when he moves up the ranks to hotter machinery.

Now Vee racing is Big Time. By placing high in major events, six Vee drivers have qualified each year since 1968 for all-expenses-paid trips to Germany in August to compete in the International Vee Championship race on the Nürburgring. There's cash money in Vee racing too. Volkswagen of America distributes $14,000 each year among individual Vee participants, not just winners. On weekends bracketing the first week of February 1970, more than $50,000 in prizes were awarded to competitors in Vee events at Daytona International Speedway. In a Zink, Jim Killion was the winner of $4050 in the first race, an SCCA event, and in a 1970 Zink Bill Scott collected $5150 for winning the second race, staged by IMSA.

Considering you can buy a race-ready Vee for $3200, or a kit for as little as $800, that't not bad.

Formula Vee, some people concluded in the mid-Sixties, was too good an idea to be left to Volkswagens alone. Saab had a go at one point with a proposed Formula S, for which some very neat Quantum cars were built in Connecticut by Hank Rudkin and Bill Kerrigan. In spite of their astonishing simplicity the Quantum Saabs were very capable race cars and a ball to drive, with the scream of a tuned two-stroke three-cylinder Saab engine ringing in your ears. Unfortunately, there never were enough Saabs around to generate a groundswell of interest in Formula S.

Neither has it been all that easy with Formula Ford. By that is meant that a Formula Ford car uses only a Ford engine, not the many suspension and gearbox parts that Formula Vee collects, and there aren't many Formula Ford competitors using engines from wrecked Ford Cortinas. But first Ford of Britain and later Ford of Dearborn got well behind the idea, working out ways to make the basic engine unit available over the counter, and now Ford's formula for fun has gone into orbit. Saab's idea wasn't so different, but it lacked full factory backing.

Formula Ford first hit the British motor racing scene on July 2, 1967, just six months after the initial plans for a new Ford-engined single-seater formula had been drafted. Originally the Cortina GT engine that formed the basis of the class was the 1500cc unit used in Ford's Cortinas prior to the present range of crossflow engines. In the early days cars to carry these engines were scarce, many of them being converted Formula 3 chassis. But this was the usual problem that confronts any new formula trying to get itself established.

By the time the 1968 season was under way, the latest 1600cc crossflow Cortina engine had appeared and had been adopted as the standard power unit for the formula. In addition racing car constructors were taking a much keener interest in the new class and, among others, Lotus, Merlyn and Russell had started producing chassis and body shells specifically for Formula Ford.

Thanks to the tremendous enthusiasm that built up among competitors, spectators and circuit owners, Formula Ford is now strongly established on the international racing scene—the formula for the up-and-coming young driver and the amateur enthusiast. The most obvious sign of this healthy growth in popularity is that more than twenty different racing car constructors are building cars specially for Formula Ford competition.

The list of builders now includes companies in Germany, Canada and the United States as well as Britain. These are some of the brand names active in Formula Ford: Lola, McNamara, Caldwell, Lotus, Dulon, Hawke, Eldon, LeGrand, Merlyn, Titan, Winkelmann, Ginetta, Palliser, Tecno, Alexis, Climax Royale, Bobsy, Nike, Piper, Fejer and Crossle. Prices for complete cars are as low as $3200, without tuned and prepared engines. For a top-class ready-to-race Formula Ford, like a fully equipped Lola, the figure will be nearer $5000.

The IMSA and SCCA rules for Ford-class cars spell out in detail the parts that can be used in the Cortina 1600 GT engines, and the extent to which they can be modified. Key dimensions and weights are strictly controlled. Stock-type single Weber carburetor is required, and a stock intake manifold, but the exhaust manifold is completely free. Obviously there are many tricks to selecting, treating and preparing the pieces of these tough, big-bore, pushrod engines.

An important difference between British and American F/F rules concerns wheels and tires. In Britain road-type steel wheels of fixed size are required, as are stock street-type tires. American rulemakers threw out the tire requirement, allowing racing tires to be used, but kept the wheel size of 13 inches with a 5½-inch rim width. SCCA calls for steel stock-type wheels, allowing offset of the center section to the rim, while IMSA allows any type of wheel construction.

There is a minimum weight limit of 400 kg. (881.6 lbs.), and the drive must be through the rear wheels only. Four-wheel drive is banned, as are limited-slip differentials and five- or six-speed gearboxes. In construction, any form of semi-monocoque is forbidden, the regulations stipulating that chassis construction must be tubular, with no stress-bearing panels except for a single bulkhead and the

The Merlyn Mark IIA is the 1969 version of the successful car used by Tim Schenken, Formula Ford's leading driver in 1968.

undertray, which is not permitted a curvature of more than 1 inch.

Despite these strict regulations, there is still considerable scope for originality and innovation in the design of Formula Ford cars. The key differences lie in details of suspension layout and the degree of adjustability of suspension, spring platforms and shock absorbers. Most cars are using the Hewland gearbox, which superseded the Renault box used in early Formula Fords. Braking is another department where constructors are allowed to try their own ideas, so long as they stick to iron calipers for their disc brakes.

The greatest distinctions between the cars lie in the design and construction of the body shell and chassis. The use of airfoils and other aerodynamic aids is forbidden. This has led some constructors to produce a body design that achieves similar objectives, producing maximum downward thrust to aid traction and adhesion when the car is cornering at speed. Lotus, for instance, produced a wedge-shape Formula Ford for 1969. Basically this Type 61 reproduced

The Russel-Alexis Mark 15—produced by Alexis Cars of England—is the 1969 version of the successful Mark 14 used by Claude Bourgoignie in 1967 and which also won the Scottish championship in the hands of David Walker in 1968.

the thinking evident in the early 1968 Formula 1 Lotus with which Graham Hill won the Monaco Grand Prix. Another car designed along these lines is the Hawke, which reproduced the Indy wedge-shape pioneered by Lotus. Ray Caldwell, on the other hand, felt the wedge was little more than a styling fad, and used a more conventional outline for his Caldwell D-9, which won the Formula Ford Championship the first year it was established by the SCCA.

When Caldwell designed his Ford-powered car he took special pains to lay out its suspension geometry to make the most of the racing tires permitted in the U.S., feeling that the British chassis were more attuned to the narrower, rounder stock tires used in Europe. It seemed, eventually, to pay off, for the Caldwell was a convincing Championship winner at Daytona in the hands of New Englander Skip Barber, who later joined the Autodynamics staff.

In only a few years Formula Ford has leaped from a promising beginner's class to a full-fledged professional circuit. Over the 1969-70 winter season, for example, Ford races posted some rewarding purses. In November at Talladega Nils Sanborn collected $1000 for a win in his Merlyn after a 100-mile IMSA event. December at Sebring under SCCA sanction saw Bill Scott awarded $1500 for a Climax-Royale victory, and at Daytona in February Jim Clark came home first in a Caldwell, drawing $2300 in the IMSA-sanctioned race. Other top-level finishers in F/F events have been Jim Jenkins, Kurt Reinold and Robert Smith in Winkelmann, Merlyn and Titan cars.

IMSA, under the guidance of John Bishop, is totally devoted to professional road racing and has built its program around Formula Ford. This was recognized by Ford Motor Company when it made a contribution, for the first time in 1970, of $10,000 to the IMSA national championship point fund. "Without Ford's help and advice," said Bishop at the time of the announcement, "there would be no serious Formula Ford racing."

Money helps, but it's not the key to the broad appeal of these cigar-shaped road racers. These are cars for the racing enthusiast who wants to enjoy his sport from the track, not from the grandstand. They are simple yet sexy, tough yet sophisticated, glamorous yet relatively cheap. That's why the Vees and Fords have turned on an entire country to the attractions of one-design class racing.

Pete Lovely bought Graham Hill's Formula 1 Lotus to compete in the 1969 Continental series. His wife, Nevele, is the chief mechanic.

6 CONTINENTAL CHARGERS

Grand Prix racing is the top class of road racing, internationally known and respected. Grand Prix cars are expensive to make, buy and maintain, because the pressure for perfection is so high, and the cost of failure higher still. Because GP competition is at such a lofty level, most countries interested in road racing have developed their own lesser formulas for single-seater race cars, ones that provide stepping stones for new drivers and builders.

The European countries logically banded together under the FIA's guidance and supervision of Formulas 2 and 3, tailored to smaller sizes, up to 1600cc soon to be enlarged to 2000cc, and designed around stock-block engines of the types usually found in Europe. Formula 2 is showing lots of life with Ford, BMW and

Ferrari engines and the promise of more in the future. Australia and New Zealand have worked out their own "Tasman" formula, which caters mainly to GP cars of the expired formulas. South America has its own "Formula 1" for engines of local manufacture.

Since the revival of road racing in North America we haven't had a top-level single-seater category. In fact we were so turned on by sports cars that it took a long time before we were even interested in open-wheeled cars at all. But now we have such a class, known as Formula A, so exciting and interesting that the British have paid us the compliment of borrowing it back again as Formula 5000. And it's fought from one end of the country to the other from April through October in the thirteen-race series for the Continental Championship.

You could say that the typical Formula A car, the star performer of the Continental, is a blend of different pieces, not a "pure" racing machine. You'd say it because its engines are a cross between Trans-Am and Can-Am power units, and the chassis derive from Formula 1, Can-Am and Indy car designs. They were very much "blended" cars in the beginning and continue that way, each year more refined, more potent, and finally built from scratch, in some cases, as Formula A cars.

The cars are cocktails, all right, but they're powerful ones. Today's Formula A was a creation of the SCCA rulemakers in 1967, allowing big American engines to race in open-wheeled chassis for the first time, under SCCA sanction, since the days of the old "unlimited" class. The doom-predictors forecast, as they had for a similar proposal by Karl Ludvigsen in 1961, that the cars would be poorly and dangerously constructed and very hazardous to drive. In their first outings the Formula A cars showed only how very high the standards of driving and preparation in SCCA racing really are.

Westport (location of the SCCA headquarters) went all the way with Formula A in 1968 by giving it the responsibility for settling the Club's national driver championship, replacing the United States Road Racing Championship (USRRC) which had been doing the same thing with the Group 7 sports/racing cars. In that way they actually created a kind of racing that *does* do a better job of decid-

David Hobbs

George Wintersteen

Dick Smothers

Tony Adamowicz

ing who's the best driver. The Group 7 cars have unlimited engines, which mean that there are often big differences in power and reliability between competitors. In the Continental, all the engines have to measure 5000cc (305ci) or less, which has much more of an equalizing effect.

John Cannon

There's been a happy relationship between the 305ci limit of the Trans-Am cars and the similar limit for Formula A, for pushrod-type (no overhead cams allowed) engines made at a rate of more than 1000 per year. Formula A rules allow an engine to be brought up or down to 305ci by changing bore, stroke, or both, and permit almost unlimited modification so long as the stock heads, block and cam and bearing locations are kept.

The coming of age in America of the big-engined open-wheeled road racing car has not been without its pains of puberty. In the beginning (circa 1950) there was the "Unlimited" class, for such as George Weaver's Maseratis and Lex DuPont's Coopers. Then there were special events for 500cc Formula 3 cars, followed by a period of controversy when the SCCA dropped F/3 from its programs, thereby serving as midwife at the birth of the California-based Formula Racing Association. FRA did yeoman service in developing new cars, drivers and circuits but it proved to be too inner-directed in its interests to advance single-seater racing to national, professional status.

Late in the Fifties Formula Junior made its bow. For several years it enjoyed wide popularity, but rapid progress in racing car design caused it to be denounced bitterly later as the "Car of the

Month Club." Nevertheless it introduced many drivers to the delights of single-seaters. During the Junior era there was also agitation for a "Formula Senior" which would be based on 1600cc stock-block engines. It failed at the time, only to be revived in the form of the current Formula B. And Formula A, through 1967, was essentially the same as the FIA Formula 1 for Grand Prix cars.

It was in 1965 that the SCCA moved to cast out Formulas Libre and Junior and to replace them with Formulas A, B and C. They enjoyed reasonable popularity through 1966, then took on dramatic new life in 1967 with the announcement of a Grand Prix Championship series of five professional races for formula machinery. Each event carried a minimum purse of $5000. First place paid $1200, second $700 and third $500. The scale diminished from there to $50 for each finisher from sixteenth through twenty-fifth place. A point system was established to determine a Champion in a series which, when all the awards were added up, totaled $27,000 in prizes.

Professionalism, points and special events attracted many more

John Cannon's Hogan-Starr McLaren leads Ron Grable's Lola at the 1970 Dallas Continental, won by Gus Hutchison.

Gus Hutchison won two races in 1970 in his Formula 1 Lotus 49.

and finer cars to the series in 1967. Paradoxically the Formula B cars proved by far the fastest, with Gus Hutchison's Lotus Ford winning four out of the five events to give the Texan the Championship. The B and C cars were well represented but A was not too popular. Chuck Kirkbride won the class in his Lotus at the Daytona Runoffs, for example, because the other three A cars entered retired. So an enlarged Formula A was instituted for 1968, following which the interest in Formula SCCA skyrocketed.

For '68 the prize fund took a giant leap upward to $91,000 spread over eight races. This was incentive enough to attract fields of as many as thirty-eight starters. No race was flagged off that year with less than twenty-eight on the grid. In spite of the expectation that the attrition would be high, especially among the big-engined Formula A cars, three out of every five starters, on the average, came through to the finish.

One of the most popular Formula A cars that first season was the Lola Type 140. Developed in consultation with the Lola American distributor, Carl Haas, the 140 was built with a tubular frame and a suspension that used some parts from the popular and successful Type 70 sports/racing Lola. This helped keep the price down, well below $10,000 without engine but with gearbox, so the rugged Lolas accounted for a high share of the starters.

The Lola 140s were runners but not winners. In only one of the eight '68 races did the British car cross the line first, Jerry Hansen's model at his home circuit, Elkhart Lake. Otherwise the Lolas were place and show machines, garnering enough points for Bob Brown to be third, Jerry Hansen fourth, Brian O'Neil fifth, Hank Candler sixth and John Gunn eighth in the end-of-season standings.

Another builder, an American this time, drew on his sports/racing experience to make cars for the new Formula A. Bob McKee of Palatine, Illinois, built several very sanitary tube-framed cars out of Armco steel. They were good enough to win a tenth spot in the Championship for Mak Kronn, who only took part in three of the qualifying events, and seventh place on points for Kurt Reinold, who was one of the first Formula A racers to experiment with a rear-mounted wing.

But the class of the 1968 Formula A field was a car born and bred in Santa Ana, California, reworked by Briton Tony Southgate from an original design by Briton Len Terry, the AAR Eagle brought to life by Dan Gurney. All American Racers was quick to realize the potential of the new Formula A, and laid down riveted monocoque shells for a series of road racing Eagles derived from the successful Indy car design.

With a structure that took much longer to make, the Eagles were also much tougher on the pocketbook, listing at $15,000 without engine or gearbox. With Wynn's sponsorship the Smothers Brothers team bought one for Dr. Lou Sell to drive. Philadelphian George Wintersteen also acquired one. Both were well maintained but the Wintersteen car was so immaculate, so beautiful it was almost embarrassing to look at. It was kept concours-ready at all times by chief mechanic Bill Mayberry.

Between them, Sell and Wintersteen monopolized the victory circles in the 1968 Continental. The only top contender to start all eight races, Sell won five, leaving two for Wintersteen. But it was indicative of the still-young status of the Championship that Sell earned only $13,700 for his efforts. Next year the winner of the second-string Formula B Championship would do just about as well.

Lou Sell, seriously injured in a late-'68 accident, wasn't able to defend his title in 1969. But another Eagle-mounted driver, a newcomer to the big cars, got the job done instead: Tony Adamowicz of Wilton, Connecticut, who had shown his skill in Porsches in the 2000cc Trans-Am class. Tony collected the crown with a margin of only one point over David Hobbs, one of the Europeans who had come to the U.S. to pick up a dollar or two. Hobbs did so very effectively, winning $27,750 in only six of the season's thirteen races, actually collecting $425 more than the Champion, Adamowicz! He did it by winning the August race at Donnybrooke and then the last three events in the series, including the relatively rich Sebring race on December 28.

For Adamowicz the middle part of the '69 season was most satisfying, with wins at Kent and Road America (Elkhart Lake) and some seconds and thirds that paid off well. Tony's Eagle was set up conservatively with a Chevy engine and parts the team was sure would work, a strategy that can be effective in a series as long as the Continental. For the last race at Sebring he tried a radical new

The Smothers Brothers Team bought an Eagle for Dr. Lou Sell to run in the 1968 series, which he handily won.

Ford engine, going for broke—and broke.

Early season favorites John Cannon and Sam Posey also chose Eagles for their Continental challenges. Cannon usually either won or blew, scoring three victories and placing fifth on end-of-season points. Posey's beautifully prepared car was wrecked in the first race, leaving him in a catch-up situation all year long as he switched to a McLaren M10A, a new monocoque car that proved able to outbrake the Eagles, until AAR came through with new front suspension uprights that allowed stronger brakes to be used on the California-built cars. Posey nevertheless salvaged third place in the Championship, helped by wins at Laguna Seca and in the second of two races held at Lime Rock.

In a surprising move, George Wintersteen changed to a car that hadn't even been a big winner in '68, the new version of the Lola designated Type 142, still with a tubular frame. With no wins, but with high finishes in eight of the thirteen races, George collected enough points for fourth in the Championship.

A Lime Rock win in '69 was scored by Peter Gethin, a British invader with a McLaren M10A, actually an unofficial representative of the McLaren factory. Gethin figured strongly in 1970 racing, with the revised M10B McLaren, starting out the year with wins in

Mike Everly, 1969 and 1970 champion in Formula B, began the 1970 season with six straight wins.

the British Formula 5000 series. As a proven design the M10B is a difficult one to beat. Those trying to do so will have a Surtees TS5A, the type of car David Hobbs used so well in '69, or a Lola Type 190, an all-new machine with a monocoque frame, or a Leda, the latest from Len Terry's drafting board, sold and serviced in the U.S. by All American Racers.

Ford and Plymouth engines are starting to make their presence known in the Continental cars, dating from Sebring, 1969. Young Swede Savage put a Plymouth-powered Eagle on the pole there, with an engine prepared by the Zeus Development Company of Wayne Jones. Hiroshi Fushida, a talented young Japanese driving star, is now handling this car well in the series. Like other up-and-coming drivers, Fushida feels Formula A will give him a chance to gain experience at high speed, plus lots of exposure to influential people in racing.

Otherwise, Chevy remains king in Formula A. The evergreen Z28 units are race-prepared by many able crews including Traco Engineering, Al Bartz, Louie Unser and Ryan Falconer. Each has its own preference for components. Ignition can be coil or magneto. Induction can be Weber carbs or fuel injection by Lucas, Bosch or modified Hilborn. Crankshaft can have a conventional 90-degree angle between throws or can be a "flat" 180-degree type as pioneered in this class of racing by Al Bartz and John Cannon in 1969. Whatever the combination, it still seems to take a Chevy to win, in either Formula A or the similar Formula 5000.

As for engine weight, there's not much the builders can do until somebody like Ford or Chevrolet decides to mass-produce a small-displacement V8 with an aluminum block. Such an engine would make it easier to get down to the 1250-pound minimum weight for 305ci cars. Formula A also permits you to run an all-out unrestricted racing engine with as many camshafts as you want, but it has to be 3000cc (183ci) or less. You're cut back to a 26-gallon fuel tank, but you can also build a lighter car, down to 1105 pounds.

Formula A engines are a cross between Trans-Am and Can-Am power units, with chassis derived from Formula 1.

These statistics allow a pure Formula 1 Grand Prix car to compete, like the Lotus Type 49 of Pete Lovely or the Brabham of Gus Hutchison, powered by a Cosworth Ford V8. In the U.S., far from the British plant that built it, such an engine is at a disadvantage. It produces 425 horsepower at high revs, while a good Chevy should produce 510 or so, at a lower peak speed and with a better torque curve. Laden with fuel and driver the 305ci car would have 3.4 pounds for each horsepower to push, less than the 3.6 pounds per horsepower of the GP-type car. It's a close match, weighted against the 183ci engine.

If Chevy dominates Formula A, Ford does likewise in Formula B/C. This was made possible back in 1962 when free-lance designer Harry Mundy produced a new twin-camshaft cylinder head for the British Ford four-cylinder engine, the unit that's still used in the Cortina today. Lotus makes them and other firms, BRM and Vegantune, prepare them for racing in the 1600cc (97ci) size required by Formula B. Lucas fuel injection is indispensable for success in "B," for an engine mounted in a top Brabham or Lotus chassis.

In 1969 Formula B was the personal property of Mike Eyerly of Seattle, Washington. The son of Harry Eyerly, who used to dominate Class H just as completely in his formidable Crosley specials, Mike crushed his competition with a string of six victories and two second-place finishes in the first nine races. He had more than twice the points of the second-place man in the standings, Fred Stevenson. Fred handled a Lotus, while Eyerly drove a Brabham BT18.

The Continental Championship entered the decade of the Seventies on a new wave of wealth. The promoters of the thirteen events in '70 promised to put up a minimum of $20-25,000 per race, for a total series purse of $300,000—well up from 1969's $244,000. In addition, Liggett & Myers, Inc. posted L&M Winners Circle awards totaling $110,000. At each race, the top three drivers in both Formula A and Formula B sliced up a $5000 award melon. Awaiting the top points winners at the end of the season—in Formula A only—is a $40,000 bonus jackpot covering the top ten drivers, with $10,000 going to the Champion.

In his first year of open-wheeled competition, Tony Adamowicz won the 1969 Continental championship in Marv Davidson's Eagle.

Jim Kaser, SCCA director of professional racing, said of the new arrangement, "L&M's concept is a major breakthrough. We're extremely pleased with this leading company's big and different approach to racing. The $110,000 in direct cash to competitors is a real boost for stock-block formula car racing. Of equal importance are the direct promotion dollars L&M is putting into our race organizers' hands. Topping all this with a national promotional campaign means the Continental is suddenly one of the biggest auto racing series anywhere."

Whether the Continental is *really* big—big enough to attract major press coverage and public interest—will depend on its ability to draw "name" drivers and the crowds that follow them. Understandably USAC isn't encouraging its drivers to take part in what amounts to a series in direct competition to the Championship Trail. But the L&M support has, indeed, put Formula A in the big time. It's bidding to be strong enough to rank as an end in itself, not just as a means to an end.

Through the esses on the first lap of the 1967 Rex Mays 300, Gurney leads Jim Clark, Bobby Unser, John Surtees, A. J. Foyt and Mario Andretti. Dan went on to win the first Indy-car race in California since 1936.

7 INDY CARS TURN RIGHT TOO

Sports car racers and the Indy fraternity never did mix. The only thing they've had in common is mutual contempt. Now, after ten years of co-existence, the old fixed attitudes are beginning to soften. Oval racers and road racers are starting to get along with each other. Respect has improved their attitudes, respect for the successes of Dan Gurney, Mark Donohue and Peter Revson in USAC competition and those of Parnelli Jones, A. J. Foyt and Mario Andretti on the road courses. It's not One World yet, but at least we're moving in that direction.

Back in the early Fifties there were a few driver interchanges between road and oval racing. Bob Sweikert and Pat O'Connor both tried endurance racing at Sebring, having more luck than John

Al Unser

Dan Gurney

Mario Andretti

A. J. Foyt

Fitch did in trying to crack the starting lineup at Indy. Troy Ruttman made some West Coast appearances on airport circuits with a DeSoto-powered Kurtis. After the Monza 500 in 1958, when the Indy cars went to the banked track in Italy to compete with European teams, Ruttman stayed over there to race, without distinction, a 250F Maserati in a few Grand Prix events.

Still, 1958 was a milestone year for USAC's hesitant progress toward road racing. It was the first year of the organization's Road Racing Division, with four events that gave the first crown to Dan Gurney, then just making his first big move in professional racing with Frank Arciero's Ferrari. Dan was second in the year's big event, called the United States Grand Prix for Sports Cars and held at Riverside in October, with the backing of the Los Angeles Times-Mirror Company. With the then-incredible purse of $13,900, the 200-miler saw forty-two starters and a tremendous duel between Chuck Daigh in a Scarab and Phil Hill in a very special 4100cc Ferrari. Daigh took the win and the $5000 first prize in an event that was hailed, correctly, as marking the arrival of professional road racing in America.

USAC would later spurn the sports cars and turn the Riverside event back to an SCCA that had begun to realize that it could promote races for money as well as for trophies. But history of another kind had been written earlier in '58 by USAC at Riverside. The lead-off event in the season's National Midget Championship had been held on the 2½-mile California road course, on January 19. Johnnie Tolan won the 100-mile event at an average speed of 87.55 mph in a midget, a tall, one-gear-only race car with a 110ci Offy engine, owned by Bill Krech. These classic little racers, unchanged in shape since prewar days, raced at Riverside again the day after Memorial Day. The win went to Allen Heath at 83.79 mph over 500 miles.

There were no road course events on the midget calendar in 1959. But a midget made news on a road course that year, in the seventh of the fourteen races counting toward the USAC Road Racing Championship. The date was July 25, the place Lime Rock Park, Connecticut, with its 1.53-mile asphalt surface, an 80-mph track with five right-hand turns and one to the left. Sponsorship by the *New York Mirror* had drawn everything from a Formula 1 Grand Prix Maserati to a Porsche RS to northwest Connecticut for three heats of twenty, twenty and sixty laps.

A crowd of 10,000 came to the lovely Lime Rock hillside to watch, at that time a record. Among the familiar sports cars, the Maserati 300S of Pedro Rodriguez and the 4200cc Aston Martin six of the genial lap record holder, George Constantine, they saw some odd-looking racers: four Offy-powered midgets. Duane Carter, Russ Klar, Bert Brooks and Rodger Ward were the nominated drivers. The quaint-looking midgets were regarded as interesting additions to the field but hardly likely to offer competition to John Fitch in a Cooper Monaco or Chuck Daigh in a Grand Prix Maserati.

Before qualifying was over competitors and spectators were slack-jawed at Ward's 1:04.67 lap, under the track record and a second quicker than Constantine's Aston. The combination of Ward, fresh from a win at Indy, and the eleven-year-old Kurtis-built midget owned by Ken Brenn of Warren, New Jersey, was an entirely new one. Ward had contacted Brenn at the suggestion of Tony Bettenhausen, who'd driven the car and knew it was a good one. But when Brenn received a message that Rodger Ward wanted to drive the car he thought somebody was pulling his leg!

Brenn didn't change his car radically for the race. He fitted it with a foot brake instead of the usual hand brake. He accelerated work on a new high-torque engine setup he'd been planning, to have it ready for Lime Rock. Having geared the car low, in consultation with Ward, to get the best acceleration out of the turns, Brenn raised the gearing after the first heat to save the engine when it became clear that the midget had enough performance to win the race.

Constantine was the first-heat winner by only two seconds after a hard fight with the Ward midget. Judging the second-heat rolling start better, Ward took the lead, lost it to the Aston, then got it back again to win by three seconds. Ward had been pacing himself, taking it easy on the midget-size brakes, never running harder than he had to. This paid dividends in the ninety-mile final, which saw Daigh

Gordon Johncock

Roger McCluskey

Bobby Unser

The 1969 Rex Mays 300 saw a three-way battle between Gurney (48), Andretti (2) and Mark Donohue (66). It was won by Andretti when the other two broke.

and Constantine battle for the lead until the Aston Martin ground up a rear hub bearing and retired. Then Ward loitered behind Daigh's Camoradi-entered Maserati until fifteen miles from the end, when he pulled by to take the win.

This upset sent shock waves through the sports car world. "Depending on one's sentiments about road racing," Irv Dolin wrote, "it might be described as inconclusive, tragic, encouraging, unsettling, prophetic or stimulating." Commented Warren Ballard, "Ward's win was a walkaway, but many observers still wore dazed expressions of disbelief. These were no schoolboys with go-karts he'd run away from." Nor was this the first time the cool, professional Ward had raced at Lime Rock. He picked the midget as potentially winning equipment, and made his judgment look very good.

Ward kept his interest in road racing, later driving a Cooper Chevrolet sports car prepared by Bob McKee of Chicago. But there were few chances for actual USAC equipment to race on the road courses. One such chance came at Indianapolis Raceway Park, a

1.8-mile track with four turns to the right, one to the left and a ¾-mile straight. Ward brought a different midget there in July 1962, and placed second to Jim Hall's Lotus-Climax after two heats, again an excellent performance.

In July 1963, the American Racing Drivers Club staged a contest for midgets and formula cars at Lime Rock, a distinctly offbeat happening. One of the scenes that preceded it was collegiate-looking Mark Donohue, in Bermuda shorts and tennis shoes, ambling into Ken Brenn's shop and asking about a ride. Brenn and his usual driver, Len Duncan, were frankly dubious about this clean-cut apparition from the sporty car set. But when Donohue climbed into Brenn's unique rear-engined midget at Lime Rock and turned times that Duncan hadn't approached, Brenn suggested that Len might like to try on some Bermuda shorts for a change.

The first heat at Lime Rock, for midgets only, produced a win for a young Pennsylvanian who'd had some experience of road racing in his native Italy: Mario Andretti. Donohue won the longer second heat, in Brenn's latest, ahead of Brabham and Cooper Formula Juniors. In August, USAC took its midgets to the faster track at Watkins Glen, New York. Eddie Johnson was fastest qualifier and winner of the 100-mile race, ahead of Mel Kenyon and Bud Tinglestad.

In 1964 there was no action on road courses for USAC single-seaters. But other things had been happening that would pave the way for a road racing explosion along the Championship Trail. In 1961 and '62 Indy had seen the Cooper and Thompson/Buick Indy efforts with rear-engined cars, developing into the Lotus Ford programs of 1963 and '64. In the latter year American builders like A. J. Watson and Ted Halibrand made their first attempts to master this new rear-engined, independently suspended state of the art. And Jack Brabham brought to Indy his Offy-powered car that has served since as the suspension design pattern for many successful cars, including Mario Andretti's Hawks.

Either made by builders abroad, like Lotus and Lola, or following their design principles, these new USAC cars were readily adapted to road racing. It was relatively easy, compared to the old roadsters, to install multi-speed gearboxes, beef up the brakes and dial in suitable suspension settings. Experts freely predicted this was likely to happen, but it took longer than they expected to stage the first USAC Championship event on a road course. It was close to home, at Indianapolis Raceway Park, on July 25, 1965, the 150-mile Hoosier Grand Prix.

Predictably, this pace-setting race was dominated by the new "funny cars" of USAC. The top five finishers were rear-engined. Classical roadsters managed only three places in the top ten. Driving a Ford-powered Brawner-built Hawk, the winner at IRP was Mario Andretti, scoring his first victory on the Championship Trail, his first big-time win. Mario stole the race from Foyt, whose Coyote Ford ran out of gas on the last lap and fell from first to fourth. Bobby Unser's Offy was second and Roger McCluskey's Ford third. Mario repeated as winner at IRP in 1966, when it remained the sole road race on the Trail, on the way to his second USAC Championship.

Attendance at the '66 running of the Hoosier Grand Prix had been less than inspiring: fewer than 5000 people had found the race

Mario Andretti (2) started on the pole at the 1968 IRP race, but finished second in both heats. Joe Leonard drove the STP Turbocar (60).

Al Unser (15) pursues brother Bobby at the 1969 Rex
Mays. Al overtook Bobby eight laps from the end to
finish second.

worth watching. The 1967 race at IRP was to be the last, unless
attendance picked up. Meanwhile, Indy-type cars made their Canadian road course debut at Mosport, northeast of Toronto. The first
of two 100-mile heats on the July 1 card saw Bobby Unser in front,
Roger McCluskey second and Gordon Johncock third, all with Ford
power. The second heat was rained out after fourteen miles.

Andretti, who had spent most of the Mosport race in the pits,
made up for it by winning the Hoosier road race three weeks later.
After 150 miles he had a four-second margin over Al Unser, with
Bobby Unser third. The crowd of 13,500 pleased the promoters
enough to keep the event on the IRP calendar. In August the USAC
crews went back to Canada, to St. Jovite, for the Labatt 200. Andretti bested A. J. Foyt in both the 100-mile heats, Ford against
Ford. Ronnie Bucknum placed third in the first heat and Lloyd
Ruby took over that spot in the second heat.

The '67 season was open, the Championship still undecided with

Andretti, Foyt and Johncock able to win it, before the closing event in late November. It was a brand-new affair at Riverside, the first time Indy cars had raced in that state since 1936. As the "Rex Mays 300" it was named for a Californian who had been one of America's finest-ever race drivers. The race was won by a man who answers the same description in the present tense, Dan Gurney, in his own Eagle car with his own Eagle Ford engine. It was Gurney's first race for a new sponsor, Ozzie Olson.

To win, Gurney had to survive a balky clutch, a flat tire, several protests, Jim Clark, who lunched his engine, and Mario Andretti, who ran out of gas three laps from the end while in the lead. Thus Mario handed the Championship to a startled, car-hopping Foyt, who back in fifth place had not believed his luck of Indy and Le Mans in that great year could still be with him. Meanwhile Gurney was counting $31,500 in prizes for a race he was to win again in 1968.

It was a wild season, in '68, with six road races along the Trail, and with Bobby Unser, Dan Gurney, A. J. Foyt, Al Unser and Mario Andretti in a position to win any one of them, if they could stay ahead of the whistling STP Turbocars. Bobby collected the first

Dan Gurney leads the field at the start of the 1970 IRP race, only this time there's a difference—he's driving the pace car.

one in March at Las Vegas, ahead of Mario in a 150-mile race. Their unblown Ford four-cam engines fitted the normal kit for USAC road racing.

Only two weeks after Indy the Trail led to Mosport, Ontario, where Andy Granatelli entered one of his Lotus Turbocars in a road race for the first time. But in practice Graham Hill lost control of the radical machine and bent it badly. Using one of his 305ci stock-block engines again, Gurney controlled both 100-mile heats to defeat Andretti, second, and Bucknum, third. On July 7 another milestone was marked: Driven by Art Pollard, one of the STP Turbocars, supposedly so formidable that it was handicapped out of existence in 1969, actually finished a race, *for the first time.* It happened at Continental Divide Raceway, where Foyt won ahead of Lloyd Ruby. Pollard was well back in fifth place with the turbine.

The next event was historic too, with respect to another innovation that was soon to be banned by USAC. At IRP in July Al Unser drove his Lola Ford into the record books as the first four-wheel-drive car to win a road race in America. The younger Unser simply outran Andretti, second in two heats, and Foyt, third overall. Mario got some of his own back at St. Jovite in August, winning both 100-mile heats with ease.

Again the Championship came down to the wire to be settled in the Rex Mays 300, between Bobby Unser and Mario Andretti. Ahead of this showdown Dan Gurney was the winner, holding off an early challenge from Mark Donohue's Eagle Chevy, which broke its right front suspension. Andretti led Bobby until an engine blew, then headed for the pits to take over one of the two STP Turbocars in the race, hoping to pile up some more points toward the Championship.

All season, the wedge-shaped Lotuses with Pratt & Whitney power had been in trouble with brakes, especially acute on the road courses. These cars now had *eight* disc brakes apiece, two sets inboard and two outboard at both ends of the four-wheel-drive chassis. This was better, but still not great. And Mario had never, until this day, driven a turbine car in competition. He started off gingerly but was flying at the end of the back straight on his first lap—too fast to be able to brake to avoid another car that was approaching turn nine also. Who was it that Mario hit, bouncing both cars off the wall and out of the race? Why, Art Pollard in Andy Granatelli's other Turbocar, that's who. Mario climbed into yet another car but at the checker lacked just eleven points of equaling Unser's Championship-winning total of 4330.

Depending on how you look at it, the '69 season marked a step either forward or to the rear for road racing of the colorful, potent USAC single-seaters. The Trail gave up the two Canadian events—but replaced them with excellent American ones—and lost one track, Las Vegas, which folded.

As well as new courses, 1969 brought new winners to USAC's twisty-track races. Gordon Johncock's Ford-powered Gilmore Eagle won the 150-miler at Continental Divide, Colorado, in July. Gordon had to outdrive Gurney, Andretti and Al Unser to do it, which he did. Dan kept second and Foyt finished third. Another first-time winner went into the books at IRP, where Peter Revson placed third in the first heat and won the second to claim first overall. Revson's win was also the first in USAC for Repco-engined Brabham.

Traditional victors gained control in the season's three remaining races on road courses. At Donnybrooke, Minnesota, one of the new tracks on the list, an excellent three-mile facility, Gurney was completely in charge. In spite of running out of gas in the first heat, placing second, Dan won overall. Gurney was not in the picture in the next race, at Kent, Washington, a rainy episode in USAC history that saw Andretti win the first heat and Al Unser the second, for the aggregate victory. Mario was ranked second overall.

Placed third at Kent, thanks in part to the rain, was a surprising combination: New Englander Sam Posey in a Plymouth-powered four-wheel-drive STP-Lotus wedge with a three-speed automatic transmission. Though occupied at the time in chasing the SCCA Continental Championship (Chapter 6), the inquisitive Posey took a busman's holiday to find out what four-wheel-drive was like. He discovered what the Grand Prix experimenters were discovering: that a four-wheel-driver is extremely hard to steer if its front wheels are transmitting any useful power. But in view of USAC's ban, and

Swede Savage at the wheel of Gurney's Eagle Ford (48) passed Al Unser for the lead at the 1970 IRP race until A. J. Foyt (7) got by to take first.

SCCA's in the closely comparable Continental, four-wheel-drive knowledge is only of academic value now.

The STP-Plymouth cars were not competitive in the 300 miles of Rex Mays at Riverside, a long race, long enough for Mario Andretti to overcome wheel hub problems and wait out the frailties of the other leaders, Dan Gurney (faulty differential) and Mark Donohue (cracked Chevy cylinder head). Al Unser was second, and Gurney managed to salvage third.

With five road races on the list, all in America, the '70 USAC schedule was even more twisty than before. Texas International replaced Kent. Maybe some day Lime Rock will be back on the USAC calendar. It seems a long time ago, that race between Rodger Ward, George Constantine and Chuck Daigh. George is no longer with us, and the others are no longer racing. But they'd be on the mind of anyone with a memory if the USAC cars should go road racing at Lime Rock, where a midget showed that oval trackers could turn both ways—and well.

Former World Motorcycling Champion John Surtees reverts to the two-wheel method once again to get top speed out of his BRM at the 1969 Grand Prix of the United States.

8 GRAND PRIX OF AMERICA

There are many kinds of road races, from sedans to Indy cars and Formula Vees. Each has its own special attraction. Some showed tremendous promise, great spectator appeal, and soon the obituaries were being written for Grand Prix racing:

"It's too expensive today to make the cars and run the teams, and the sponsors aren't interested any more."

"Grand Prix racing is too dull. The cars are so small, and you can't see the drivers."

"The cars are too much alike. One engine is winning all the races."

In spite of all these illnesses Grand Prix racing is healthier than ever. Each season seems to crowd more events onto the calendar of

GP races counting toward the World Championship for drivers, and behind the scenes there are more tracks and nations negotiating for future dates. They'll have to go a long way to match the money standard set by the Grand Prix of the United States, with its total purse of more than $250,000.

For quite a while it seemed we'd never have a Grand Prix of the U.S. The name of GP racing reflects its origin in France in 1906, meaning literally "big prize." Precise rules were set up to define the kind of car that could compete, setting the pattern for today's Grand Prix "formula" governing car eligibility.

Actually America was the first to stage major races outside France for the massive chain-drive machines that contested the early Grand Prix events. In 1908, 1910 and 1911 Savannah, Georgia, played host to The Grand Prize Race of the Automobile Club of America, the spiritual predecessor of today's U.S. Grand Prix. (Karl Ludvigsen, one of the contributors to this book, fought a losing battle for the restoration of the name "Grand Prix" when he was the editor of *Car and Driver*.)

These were, of course, road races, as were the Vanderbilt Cup events that dated from 1904. That inaugural event was termed by Henry Austin Clark "the first really good road race in America," over a thirty-mile track on Long Island. The winner was an American, George Heath, in a French Panhard. The last race for the original Vanderbilt Cup was in 1916, won by Dario Resta's Peugeot at Santa Monica.

With the construction of the Indianapolis Motor Speedway, and the emergence of the board tracks of the Twenties, America lost interest in road racing. It was revived on an amateur basis during the Thirties by the Automobile Racing Club of America. A new Vanderbilt Cup was commissioned for races in 1936 and 1937 on an artificial road circuit on Long Island, Roosevelt Raceway. Tazio Nuvolari won the first one with an Alfa Romeo, Bernd Rosemeyer the second with an Auto-Union from Germany.

During the Thirties Germany had tremendously expanded the scope and importance of Grand Prix racing by using it as a political

Graham Hill   Jim Clark

Jack Brabham   John Surtees

instrument, and Fascist Italy hadn't been far behind. GP racing was resumed in 1946, and in 1950, for the first time, the point system for the driver's World Championship was established. Even though the Indy "500" no longer conformed to the GP formula (It did from 1938 through 1941), it was included as the American event counting toward Championship points. This caused such apparent oddities as a tie among Tony Bettenhausen, Jean Behra and Luigi Musso for ninth in Championship standings in 1955.

In 1958 Indy was dropped from the points list, and in the following year an audacious man, Alec Ulmann, announced in March, at the prizegiving for his twelve-hour race at Sebring, that he'd stage the first postwar American Grand Prix race at Sebring in December. That eighteen cars were on the starting grid in central Florida on December 12, 1959, for an exciting battle that would settle that year's Championship, will always stand to the credit of Alec Ulmann and his wife Mary.

That '59 U.S. Grand Prix was a colorful and exciting race. Even though it was right at the end of the season it was well supported, because Britons Tony Brooks (Ferrari) and Stirling Moss (Walker Cooper Climax) were neck-and-neck with Australian Jack Brabham (factory Cooper Climax) for the World Championship. Jack ended up with the laurels because Moss retired and Brooks fell back after a first-lap smash into a teammate. Brabham was leading to the last lap when he ran out of gas, letting young Bruce McLaren through to a surprise victory in a sister car. Jack pushed his car over the line to finish fourth, commenting, "They should have built a rope on the front end of that machine."

Before the start there was a fracas on the starting grid as Harry Schell tried to push his private Cooper Climax up to the front row of the lineup, displacing the Brooks Ferrari. Schell, a handsome and ebullient Franco-American who liked nothing better than a good practical joke, proved that he had indeed turned a very quick time, one the official scorers had ignored because it looked *too* good. No one was able to prove that Harry had done what many then suspected: At the back of the sparsely observed airport circuit he took a short cut between the rubber cones that marked the Sebring track,

Jochen Rindt

Jackie Ickx

Jackie Stewart

then waited just long enough to get going again to produce a believably quick time! It was typically Schell, and it almost certainly happened that way.

There were other colorful entries in this first revival of Grand Prix racing in America. Alejandro de Tomaso drove a GP car of his own manufacture, with an OSCA engine. A space-frame Connaught was entered, as was a Maserati-based hybrid called the Tec-Mec—both making their one and only Grand Prix appearance. American ingenuity was represented by the entry by Bob Wilke of a stretched Offy-powered midget driven by Rodger Ward, who juggled with two shift levers and a brake lever while sliding the racer around the unfamiliar turns. Rodger was last on the grid and an early retirement with clutch trouble.

Alec Ulmann didn't try to hide the fact that his Grand Prix in central Florida was a financial disaster. But he was able to keep the race date in 1960, and he took the U.S. GP far west to Riverside. Then the center of professional road racing in the U.S., Riverside seemed to offer the best chance to run a Grand Prix that would draw enough spectators to pay its own way. Ulmann's organization, however, failed to woo successfully the all-powerful sports writers

Alec Ulmann staged the first Grand Prix of the United States at Sebring on December 12, 1959. It was won by Bruce McLaren in a Cooper Climax.

Emerson Fittipaldi, from Brazil, surprised everyone when he won the 1970 U.S. Grand Prix in a Lotus.

and editors on the Los Angeles papers, so there was practically no local prerace buildup—and another financial catastrophe.

Even though the World Championship had been settled, with another award to Brabham, the race was attended by every major team except Ferrari. Brabham took an early lead with his Cooper Climax, the rear-engined car that had revolutionized Grand Prix racing, but fell back with a fuel leak fire and finished fourth. From the fifth lap to the finish Stirling Moss took command in one of the two identical dark blue Lotus Climaxes Rob Walker had brought to Riverside for him.

Two relative newcomers to the Lotus factory team, Jim Clark and John Surtees, locked horns early in the race and dropped out of contention. Riverside's own Dan Gurney was a strong challenger in the rear-engined BRM but had, as usual, engine trouble. Holding fifth spot through all but the last lap, placing seventh with a failing transmission, was Texan Jim Hall. His Lotus Climax was a do-it-yourself conversion of a Formula 2 model "that was, as luck would have it, a very good car," Hall later recalled.

West-Coasters Pete Lovely and Bob Drake also entered in over-matched equipment, placing out of the first ten. Tenth place at the flag was occupied by a very happy race driver, Chuck Daigh, in the front-engined Scarab. This was the only *Grande Epreuve* (a race counting for World Championship points) this American-made car was ever to finish. Daigh and Phil Remington had lightened and simplified it before the race, and found during the event that it quit the oil-blowing that had always plagued its desmodromic-valved four-cylinder engine. They theorized afterward that for the first time it had run long enough to get the rings properly seated!

The 1960 race had been the last chance for the Scarab, for it was the final event run under the Grand Prix Formula 1 that had been established in 1954 and modified in 1958. Now, in 1961, a new and extremely controversial Formula 1 was taking effect, one that would force the design and construction of entirely new cars. Who decided what the new formula would be? Such decisions are made by the Fédération Internationale de l'Automobile, an international association of motoring clubs based in Paris. By vote, the FIA adopts or rejects the recommendations of the Commission Sportive Internationale, the sporting committee that's responsible for approving cars, setting the racing calendar and proposing changes in regulations.

From 1954 through 1960 the Formula 1, the designation of the premier formula usually (but not always) used for Grand Prix racing, permitted supercharged cars of up to 750cc or 45ci and unblown engines of up to 2500cc or 152ci. There was an important change of pace in 1958 when fuels were limited to aviation gasoline instead of the free choice that had been possible before. Then, concerned about speed and safety, the CSI proposed and the FIA adopted for 1961 a formula that cut the engine size back to 1500cc or 91ci unblown and imposed a minimum weight to encourage the construction of stronger cars.

This 91ci limit was exceedingly unpopular with the British, who

Colin Chapman throws his hat in the air as Jochen Rindt takes the 1969 U.S. GP.

Jackie Ickx had an engine failure and parked his Brabham Ford off course at the 1969 U.S. GP.

had found themselves doing well toward the end of the previous
formula and didn't want to change the status quo. Yet they finally
buckled down to the job of building new cars—so effectively that
every U.S. Grand Prix run under the 91ci formula, through 1965,
was won by a British car and driver.

Now, however, there was a new location for America's only
World Championship race. Back in 1958, Cameron Argetsinger of
Watkins Glen, New York, the town that had hosted the rebirth of
road racing in America ten years earlier, decided to try something
new. He staged a special "formula libre" race, which means "free
formula," or, more loosely, "anything goes." In those days Grand
Prix cars were the quickest things around, so it was no surprise that
Jo Bonnier came home the winner in a GP Maserati 250F ahead of
Dan Gurney and Bruce Kessler in sports Ferraris.

In 1959 the Glen Formula Libre race made its famous run in a
snowstorm, marking one of the oddest victories in the long logbook
of Stirling Moss. His Cooper Climax was the class of a poor field.
Moss won again in 1960, this time with a Lotus Climax, against

tougher opposition from Jack Brabham, who was second, from a field that began to have the look of Grand Prix quality. With these credentials, Watkins Glen applied for and won the right to host the Grand Prix of the United States in 1961. It's been held there ever since.

In '61, for the second straight year, Ferrari elected to stay away from the U.S. Grand Prix. This time it was specially exasperating of him because it meant that Americans couldn't see their new World Champion driver, Phil Hill, in action in the car that carried him to the pinnacle he's the only American ever to have reached. The race saw Moss and Brabham fight for the lead then retire, leaving the victory to Innes Ireland and Team Lotus. Dan Gurney was second in a Porsche, and Tony Brooks third in a BRM powered by a Climax engine.

With Canadians flocking south of the border to see some world-class motor racing, and with the excellent tradition built up at the Glen, it was proving to be a fine place to hold a Grand Prix race. In fact the track and the way the race is staged ranks toward the top of the list of the members of the Grand Prix Drivers Association. In '62 there were no Ferraris again and the Moss-Brabham duel was

Mario Andretti made headlines in 1968 by qualifying first at the U.S. GP in a Lotus Ford, but a broken nose wing sidelined him early in the race.

replaced by a Jim Clark–Graham Hill battle, Clark's Lotus beating Hill's BRM. Bruce McLaren was third in a Cooper.

Graham Hill may have been second in 1962 but he was first with his BRM in 1963—and 1964—and 1965, establishing the longest winning streak in the short history of the U.S. Grand Prix. In '63 Ferrari was goaded into bringing a team of cars and almost won with the V6 of John Surtees, which retired with a broken piston when in the lead. Richie Ginther's BRM was second and Clark's Lotus was third after starting late following a battery replacement.

The mustachioed Hill's second Glen victory in 1964 saw him ahead of Surtees' Ferrari and, in a commendable third place, Jo Siffert from Switzerland in his private BRM-engined Brabham. The next year twelve-cylinder cars were entered, Ferraris for Lorenzo Bandini and Pedro Rodriguez and Hondas for Richie Ginther and Ronnie Bucknum. They were no match, though, for the winning V8 of Hill and the V8-Climax-powered Brabhams of Dan Gurney and Jack himself in second and third places. This was the next-to-last race of the 1500cc Formula 1, trailed by the GP of Mexico.

In 1966 the CSI permitted the engines to get bigger again in Grand Prix cars, apparently concluding that tires and chassis had improved enough in the meantime to make it possible to transmit and handle more power safely. Supercharged 91ci engines were permitted, but no one's tried to use one. Instead they've preferred the unblown 183ci or 3000cc limit. A minimum weight still applies, as do many other regulations for safety equipment and maximum body width. Bodywork, with the exception of fuel tanks, isn't allowed to extend laterally beyond the inner edge of each wheel, so the cars are compulsorily open-wheeled racers.

At Watkins Glen in '66 there was a new formula for the prize money as well as for the cars. Instead of the traditional starting money and token prize money package, calculated to bring a maximum number of cars to the grid but not necessarily to promote close racing, the Glen organizers split with precedent to offer a purse of more than $100,000. The $20,000 for the winner was more than the combined first prizes in all the other GP races in 1966! It was pocketed that year by Jim Clark, who outlasted Bandini's Ferrari

The independent Brabham of the late Piers Courage is pursued by the factory Brabhams of Jackie Ickx and Jack Brabham at the 1969 U.S. GP.

and the Brabham Repco of World Champion Jack Brabham. Clark's Lotus was powered by the BRM H16, which scored its only race victory on this occasion. Grand Prix newcomer Jochen Rindt was second and John Surtees third, both in Maserati-engined Coopers.

Watkins Glen's track, though only 2.3 miles long, is one of the faster ones in the Grand Prix series. The first over 120-mph race average was set in 1967, after a stirring battle between teammates Graham Hill and Jim Clark in matched Lotuses powered by the new Cosworth Ford V8 engine. Prodded by Chris Amon until Amon's Ferrari failed, Clark crossed the finish line with his right rear wheel at a rakish angle, his suspension broken, to take the win. Hill was second and Denny Hulme, that season's World Champion, third in a Brabham Repco.

Mario Andretti made headlines in the U.S. Grand Prix in 1968

113

The use of wings had become so widespread in 1968 that all but one car in the U.S. GP was equipped with them.

*

by setting the fastest qualifying time in his Lotus Ford, proving his tremendous skill and versatility against the world's finest drivers. It was the oddest-looking field ever to face lavender-suited starter Tex Hopkins, for every entry but one (the Piers Courage BRM) was equipped with high-flying wings. A nose wing, failing in the early laps, put Mario out of the picture, and Jackie Stewart took an easy win with his Dunlop-tired Matra Ford. It was the first U.S. Grand Prix victory by a French-made car.

Another "first" went into the record books after the '69 race, which marked Jochen Rindt's first victory in a *Grande Epreuve*. Stewart fought Rindt's Lotus Ford for the lead, but then retired, leaving second place to a batch of battling Brabhams. All Ford-powered, the factory cars of Brabham and Jackie Ickx were having trouble holding the Frank Williams-entered car of Piers Courage. Ickx retired and the young British brewery heir successfully held off

Jack Brabham, who placed fourth. Surtees brought a BRM through to a third place finish—unusual these days for this British make. Race speed was the fastest ever at 126.36 mph.

Rindt's fastest lap in '69 was 128.69 mph at Watkins Glen, slower than the lap record held by Hulme at 132.27 mph in a Can-Am McLaren Chevrolet. There's no clearer indication of the fact, obvious today, that there are other cars that are faster and sometimes more spectacular than the Grand Prix machines. But why, then, does the U.S. Grand Prix get more and more popular every year? Why is there pressure to move the race, or to obtain a second date counting for points in the U.S.?

Grand Prix cars retain a technical fascination, with competition so close that engineers try every possible trick to pull out a performance margin. That's why Can-Am specialists like McLaren still feel a need to stay active in GP racing. Also, the very tightness of the Grand Prix formula assures close competition among the drivers. There's also a Championship for the GP car maker, but it's insignificant in importance compared to the driver's World Championship that's settled by the Grand Prix circus.

Nothing in road racing matches the romantic appeal of the Grand Prix series, moving from country to country with the same cars and drivers, putting their skills on the line one weekend after another before an international audience. Luckily, in the United States we're part of that audience once a year.

Chief starter Tex Hopkins flags the 1968 Glen winner, Jackie Stewart.

Michigan International Speedway. The new look in road racing—a combination speedway/road circuit.

9 WHERE THE ROADS ARE

What it's all about is racing on roads. Sometimes it's easy to forget that's where this all started, and that actual roads are supposed to be simulated by the artificial circuits of today. Some of them seem more like the nightmares of demented civil engineers than honest, realistic highways. But in all there are one hundred tracks available for use, in a good year, by road racers in the fifty states. That's enough to keep our club and professional drivers well occupied.

Where local laws permit it, streets can still be closed off to allow road racers to ply their skills between real curbs and corners. This is usually possible only in two situations: where the road is through a park, so its closing doesn't impede normal traffic, or where it goes completely around a lake, again so it's not blocked by cross traffic.

When possible, existing roadways are used for tracks in Montgomery, Alabama, North Little Rock, Arkansas, at Burns Park, at San Diego Stadium, California, at Pomona, California, and at Hawaii Raceway Park. Kansas has two circuits around lakes, at Shawnee Lake and at Lake Afton, near Wichita. Kansas City International, Missouri, is on local roads, as is the track at Ponca City, Oklahoma.

In the Northwest real roads are raced on at Delta Park in Portland, Oregon, and Ocean Shores, Washington. And in Texas there are two such tracks, Austin Raceway Park and San Jacinto Monument in Houston. Such circuits suffer, of course, from being usable only a few times a year. They also offer crowd control problems, not the least of which is figuring out ways to charge the spectators for seeing the races. And the safety problems of trees, light poles, hydrants and buildings along the track are such that these courses couldn't be approved for major racing events.

Then there are the airports. At the opposite extreme from real roads, they offer no hazards at all except the boredom of a long, long spin or the danger of a poorly placed haybale. Of course they're also the least of all like roadways, many airport tracks suffering from dimly defined corners and pavement so abrasive it turns races into tire-testing contests. This doesn't necessarily apply to the parts of airport tracks that are made up of service roads, such as the complete back section at Sebring.

Alabama is host to two airports that are also used for road races at Courtland and Huntsville. Arizona brings an airport into action at Tucson as Arkansas does at Stuttgart, and to the west in California the Holtville airport goes racing. Sebring set the pace in Florida, where airport courses are also in use at Sebastian, Fernandina Beach and Osceola. Kansas has three, at Olathe, Hutchinson and Salina, and New Mexico has two, at Fort Sumner and Roswell.

Chennault Air Force Base at Lake Charles, Louisiana, sees road racing events on its runways. Cumberland, Maryland, is one of the veteran airport tracks among those used by the SCCA. In Oklahoma there's Stillwater, and at Edgemont, South Dakota, and Reading, Pennsylvania, airports host road racers. That's the case in Texas at San Marcos and Galveston, and in Washington at Shelton.

As interest in road racing grew enough to make it worthwhile to build special tracks for it, some of the first were made by adding a road course onto an existing oval track raceway. This was done, for example, at Thompson, Connecticut, where a third-generation track layout is now in use, at State Fair Park in West Allis, Wisconsin, and at Marlboro, Maryland, where the "Lavender Hill Mob" financed its own expansion of a tiny oval.

With all-new tracks being built, some promoters decided to hedge their bets on the future by designing facilities that could be used as ovals and road courses and even drag strips as well. One of the first of the breed was Bill France's Daytona International Speedway in Florida, big enough to hold the road section in its infield. American Raceways followed this pattern for the two tracks it completed at the end of the Sixties, Michigan International at Irish Hills and Texas International at College Station.

Other combinations of ovals and road courses took shape in Arizona, at Phoenix International, in Colorado at Continental Divide Raceway in Castle Rock, in Indiana at Indianapolis Raceway Park in Clermont and in Pennsylvania at Pocono International. This style has also been selected for the most ambitious track construction program ever attempted anywhere, the Ontario Motor Speedway in California, east of Los Angeles.

Appropriately, with year-round weather suitable for car competition, California leads the other forty-nine states by a long way in the number of permanent road circuits it offers the racing fan. Laguna Seca at Monterey, south of San Francisco, is a fiendish track whose degree of difficulty can only be appreciated from the driver's seat. Riverside Raceway at Riverside is a pioneering plant, with an unusual multi-plan track layout that's varied for SCCA or USAC or NASCAR competition. Orange County Raceway is near Anaheim, and there's also the veteran Willow Springs road course in California. A track near Sacramento is under construction.

Other western road racing circuits include Aspen Raceways in Aspen, Colorado, the challenging Seattle International at Kent, Washington, War Bonnet Park at Mannford, Oklahoma, and Portland International, Portland, Oregon. Texas has two road courses, Penwell's Odessa Raceway Park and Smithfield's Green Valley. Missouri is home to Mid-America Raceway at Wentzville, as is Tennessee to Shelby County Raceway at Memphis, and Utah to Bonneville Raceway Park at Salt Lake City. Down south, Florida offers Miami-Hollywood Speedway at West Hollywood, and Georgia boasts two permanent tracks: Road Atlanta at Douglasville and Savannah International Raceway at Faulkville. Chesapeake International Raceway is under construction at Elkton, Maryland, to a design by Mark Donohue.

Midwestern America is relatively rich in permanent road circuits of high quality. In Wisconsin, Clif Tufte's Road America, at Elkhart Lake, set a high standard for all American tracks when it opened its gates in 1956. That standard has been approached by the new Donnybrooke Speedway at Brainerd, Minnesota. There are two tracks in Illinois: Blackhawk Farms at Rockton and Illinois International at Carpentersville.

Michigan offers Grattan International, on the west side of the state, and the twisty Waterford Hills layout, northwest of Detroit. Another track known for its "tight" corners is Mid-Ohio, at Lexington. Also in Ohio is Steel Cities International, at Warren. Danville, Virginia, is home base for a veteran circuit, the 3¼-mile Virginia International Raceway. Keith Bryar's Motorsport Park is at Loudon, New Hampshire, folded on a hillside. Bridgehampton is spread over sand dunes at the tip of Long Island, New York, and the third of the various tracks that have been used at Watkins Glen lies west of the scenic New York town, criss-crossing the local highways. Tucked in the northwest corner of Connecticut is Lime Rock Park, where Rodger Ward pulled off that famous upset victory in his mighty midget.

There's not a single grandstand at Lime Rock. You watch racing there from grassy hillsides that overlook several turns and straights, the track sweeping through a lovely Connecticut valley. Elkhart Lake is much the same. Where oval tracks and road circuits are combined, as at the American Raceways circuits, there are often large stands that command a view of almost the whole course. Each arrangement presents its own special opportunities for viewing a road race.

There's a knack to watching a road race and getting the most out of it—as there is to spectating at any sophisticated sport. One of the best sets of guidelines to understanding road races was compiled by Bob Cochnar, automotive columnist for the Newspaper Enterprise Association, one of the sponsors of the American Road Race of Champions. These are the points he feels are important:

1. *Make racing a weekend event.* Although the race itself may be as short as two hours (or as long as twenty-four hours), the activities leading to the fall of the green flag on race day are also interesting. Let's assume you reach the track on a Saturday morning, the day before the race. It's wise to book hotel and motel rooms well in advance because—remember—racing is popular. At many courses, camping facilities are available in the infield or nearby at little cost.

2. *Buy the right tickets.* Unless you're race-going only for fun in the sun (this is also popular), there's no good reason to buy a grandstand ticket. A paddock or infield ticket can be more useful since it gives you the opportunity to see the cars, mechanics and drivers up close. At certain racing plants, however, a seat on an interesting corner is a good bet, though this might limit your movement.

3. *Get the lay of the land.* Saturday is usually practice and qualifying day. Drivers want to make sure their cars are set up properly for the particular circuit they're on and also to familiarize themselves with the course.

This is an ideal time for you to wander around the circuit (making sure you don't stumble into areas closed to spectators; if areas are closed it is only because they are dangerous). Observe how individual drivers negotiate corners. Watch as their taillights wink on and off, indicating braking points. Listen for the change in engine pitch as the drivers shift up and down.

4. *Sample the pit action.* An old racing axiom is that races are won and lost in the pits. Every driver brings to a race a group of dedicated, skilled men who must make sure their car is in superb

mechanical condition. A sloppy pit crew can easily lose a race for a driver. So the flurry of pitside activity is not without purpose. Every moving part is painstakingly checked, tires are switched regularly and very often you can see the insides of a car scattered on the ground, the mechanics tinkering with a malfunctioning frammis. This is ideal subject material for photographers.

5. *Find the "right" place for dinner.* All the action at a race doesn't take place on the track. In every racing town, there are a few places where drivers, officials, mechanics, racing writers, publicity men and knowledgeable hangers-on mingle. Although the drivers will leave the scene early, you can pick up considerable inside lore from the rest. Racing people are generally friendly, willing to answer questions and to convince others that their sport is "the greatest." From them, you'll find who's favored tomorrow, what shape the cars are in and who drives well and who not so well. It's all interesting, all inconclusive.

6. *Get up and out early.* Regardless of the weather, in road racing the show always goes on. Remember that the intent is to stimulate actual public-road driving conditions and people don't stop driving because of a little rain. It's best to be at the track well before noon, although major races seldom begin before 2 P.M.

You already know from which points you'll be watching the race, so it may be a good time to stroll through the public parking lots to see the exotic machinery which brings so many fans to the races. Ferraris are cheek-by-jowl with Rolls-Royces; Dodge Motor Homes share spaces with dune buggies.

And there are the race fans themselves. It is a wild mixture: hippies and English-country-squire types; young families (child papoose-like on dad's back) and elderly couples in tweedy outfits; amateur photographers laden with thousands of dollars of equipment; lissome "pit popsies" in bikinis and stopwatches.

7. *Make sure you have a program.* Race programs are much more than souvenirs; you must rely on them to find out who's driving what. One of the more valuable inclusions is the lap chart, through which you can determine who really is first, second and third. If you elect to complete a lap chart, however, it is almost

mandatory that you stake out one observation point from which you won't be able to move. During the race, as the cars roar by, you'll have to note their number in the appropriate lap box. You'll then know who is on what lap; the driver with the most laps in a given period of time (or who reaches the prescribed number of laps first) is the winner.

8. *At the start, be at the start.* Although at any other time the start/finish line is the least interesting place, when the green flag drops and the cars charge for the first turn, it's the essence of the sport and *the* place to be. The screech of racing engines at full bore coupled with the cheers of the crowd combine to create a heart-pounding moment. Whoever makes it to the corner first may well be in the leading position at the end of the lap but this is by no means assured. And that is what makes racing exciting.

9. *Begin the slow ramble.* After the first lap or two, you should hit your first observation point to see how the cars negotiate that particular turn. The drivers by now will have found their particular "groove," the line which gets them around the turn fastest without loss of control.

If you have a stopwatch, this is the time to use it. You'll be able to tell which drivers are the fastest by starting your clock as a car enters the turn and stopping it as it heads into the straight. The skillful driver can shave critical tenths of seconds here.

After you have a feeling of that viewing point, move to your next spot, and so on until you are back to the start/finish line at the closing laps.

10. *There's more than one race to watch.* First-timers may get the impression that because the leader is ten or more laps ahead of the pack, the race is as good as won and the excitement is over. But very often the more interesting racing, the more dramatic performances, are found well behind the winner. Say, for example, that a highly competitive driver is forced into the pits for a lap or two. He'll probably pull out all the stops to catch up and exhibit a breath-taking style as he threads through the traffic. The battle among several cars for second, third or any place good for championship points should also be watched.

Remember, too, that in many SCCA races two or more classes are run at the same time. This means there is really more than one race to follow and more than one eventual winner.

As you can see, there's much more to road racing than meets the eye. To understand it takes some effort on the part of the spectator. But perhaps that's why the sport is rapidly reaching new heights in popularity.

10 HOW TO LEARN TO ROAD RACE

Anyone who has a desire to race, and can manage to budget some time and money to do it, can make a start in road racing today. The first steps are moderately expensive, about as costly as getting a complete skiing outfit, plus the preparation of the car. Before you decide to attend a driver's school for road racing you'll probably have tasted the sensation of extending your car and yourself at an autocross or other "solo" speed event, so you'll have some idea whether you enjoy it or not. It's important that you enjoy it. Most people drive road racing cars because they enjoy it more than almost anything else.

As road racing becomes more and more "big business," there are more chances to do well, professionally, as a driver. But few will start racing with this as an objective. About 3500 men and women hold SCCA national driver's licenses, qualifying them to take part in top-level events, either club or professional, and automatically qualifying them to hold an FIA international license. Another 2500 hold regional licenses, making them eligible to race in the many events on the crowded regional racing calendar.

It's obvious that not all these 6000 folks are clear-eyed, steel-nerved, clean-living, dedicated professional racers. Many will never pass the regional license stage, finding out what racing is like but concluding it's not for them. Some may not graduate from driver's school, either by their own choice or that of the instructors. If you'd like to find out in relative privacy and in very expert hands whether or not you have what it takes to make the grade in road racing, consider attending a school for racers like the fine one Bob Bondurant conducts. He was originally affiliated with Orange County Raceway, near Los Angeles, and is now working with the new Ontario Motor Speedway at Ontario, California.

You'll also get an excellent grounding in the essence of road racing if you attend the school program of the SCCA. To give you an idea of what to expect, here's a check list of the things you'll have to do before you and your car will be accepted for your first driver's school:

1. Join both the Sports Car Club of America ($10 yearly dues) and the Sports Car Club region of residence.
2. Pass a thorough physical examination by an M.D. of your choice using SCCA medical forms.
3. Provide the SCCA with two passport-sized photographs.
4. Pay your region $4.50, for which you will receive a novice permit, and copies of the General Competition Rules (GCR) and the Production Car Specifications (PCS).
5. Install the following equipment on the car that you will use during the drivers' school:

   A roll bar conforming to the specifications outlined in Appendix Z of the General Competition Rules. (Approximate cost $75.)

Seat belts (both driver and passenger sides) and driver shoulder harness. See General Competition Rules, Appendix Y. (Approximate cost $30.)

Approved racing tires. See GCR, Appendix A, section 1.5.1. (Approximate cost $30-$60 per tire.)

Install an extra return spring on the carb linkage.

Replace the glass fuel filter bowl with one of metal.

Install an aproved fire extinguisher in the car. See GCR, Appendix A, section 1.5.1.-S. (Approximate cost $15.)

6. Each driver-trainee must wear:

Approved crash helmet with Snell Foundation Seal attached. (Approximate cost $40.)

Goggles or face shield. (Approximate cost: goggles $10, face shield, $5.)

Long-sleeved flame-resistant driving suit of SCCA-approved material and driving gloves. (Approximate cost: suit $30, gloves $7.)

7. The driver-trainee's car must be prepared according to the GCRs and be able to pass a rigid technical inspection before the car will be allowed on the course. See GCR, Appendix A.

All these precautions are necessary because driving school is serious business. Racing is dangerous, but the SCCA wants to keep it as safe as possible, especially for the first-timers. That's the atmosphere throughout the school: thoroughness and devotion to detail. You're urged to take it easy—yet try hard; to relax—yet think and concentrate. And don't act like you know it all, because you'll be graded on your deportment and attitude, and that of your crew as well. Instructors would like to weed out drivers whose mental attitude might endanger their own lives and the safety of others.

You'll soon find out you don't know it all, anyway. You'll be assigned an instructor who's familiar with the kind of car you're driving, and he'll have a lot of pointers about its behavior that will be very valuable. The instructor will also know all about the track where the school is conducted. You'll learn more than you ever realized could be learned about a piece of roadway as you walk all the way around it with him, examining changes in camber, differences in pavement, key cutoff points, gradient changes and locations of apexes of corners. And later, on the track, you'll put that knowledge to use, because in driver's school you're expected to show speed as well as smoothness.

Your novice permit is issued only to allow you to take part in drivers' schools. Before you can move on to actual racing events, you have to complete these school requirements first:

1. Obtain the signature of the chief steward attesting to participation at each drivers' school attended.
2. Complete total of at least six hours of in-car, on-course time at drivers' school events.
3. Complete at least two drivers' school events with a "satisfactory" rating.

After completion of drivers' school requirements, the holder of a novice permit must:

1. Participate in two regional events and obtain the signature of the chief steward attesting to satisfactory performance.
2. Complete the requirements for a regional license within a maximum of two calendar years.

A novice permit may be renewed only once, when it expires at the end of the calendar year issued. It will be renewed by the home SCCA region upon receipt of a new medical form, fee and photographs, and the old permit will be attached to the new one. If the requirements have not been completed at the expiration of the renewed license, and the holder wishes to continue, he must start over again with no credit for schooling and for regional race participation.

The chief steward of a drivers' school, or the divisional license chairman, may waive all or part of the drivers' school requirements for drivers with prior racing experience.

Holders of novice permits who have satisfactorily completed the drivers' school requirements and two regional events may apply for a regional license. These are the things they have to submit to the SCCA:

1. Novice permit with approving signature of the regional execu-

tive or his designated representative in the space provided.

2. Current medical form. Applicants may use the current medical form on file with the home region, but it must be included with the application.

3. Five-dollar regional license fee.

Refusal by the home region to approve the application may be appealed by the applicant to the divisional license chairman for his final decision.

Regional licenses are valid for a calendar year. Renewal applications will be mailed automatically. Regional license holders may apply for renewal by submitting:

1. Completed renewal application with a record of participation in at least two events during the preceding calendar year.

2. A new, completed medical form.

3. Five-dollar license fee.

Drivers who have participated in at least four events as a regional license holder within two calendar years may apply for a national license. The requirements are:

1. Regional license with record of participation in at least four events in the past two calendar years, signed by applicant. Events run as a novice do not count.

2. Current medical form. Applicants who have submitted a medical form for the current year need not submit a new one.

3. Five-dollar national license fee.

Once you have a national license, you can renew it each year if you've taken part in at least two events in the preceding year, one of which must be a national or FIA-listed event. A new medical form is also required, highlighting the Club's strict attitude toward close medical scrutiny of all participating drivers.

As an organization that stresses the fun of fast driving, the SCCA has also pioneered in the development of safety equipment for the protection of drivers, drawing on the best technology for better helmets, better suits and better restraint systems for keeping drivers in cars so they'll be better protected in an accident. This presumes that the car will have a strong roll-over bar, and it would be idle to suggest that there was not a lot of argument among Club members over the aesthetic, moral and sporting aspects of roll bars. But they were adopted, and no one would wish that it had been otherwise.

In 1956, after the untimely death of their friend Peter Snell in a roll-over accident, a group of California SCCA members decided to find out why he died, and how to prevent similar fatalities. From this initial effort the Snell Memorial Foundation was incorporated in 1958 to undertake professional research and rate various helmets on the market.

With the help of a grant, and continuing contributions from SCCA and others, intensive testing of production helmet samples was conducted. Under the direction of Dr. George S. Snively, entirely new helmet standards were formulated. The data were made available to all interested manufacturers, federal and state agencies, law enforcement bodies and consumer groups. The Foundation's seal of approval became the SCCA standard. The seal must appear on each of the thousands of helmets worn in SCCA races, from training sessions to world championships.

In 1966 the SCCA completed a five-year project to sponsor the specifications for helmets. The results were submitted to the American Standards Association, U.S. member of the International Organization for Standardization, and standard Z. 90.1 was adopted, providing a level of head gear protection previously unknown. This further standardization had the unanimous approval of an ASA committee which included representatives of helmet manufacturers, insurance companies, testing organizations, National Safety Council, International Association of Chiefs of Police, Departments of the Army and the Navy, and power boating, skiing, karting, cycle and automobile competition organizations.

During the mid-Sixties, more attention was being given to the kind of clothing a racing driver should wear. The flame-resistance of garments, then required and achieved by dipping cotton in a solution, was being radically improved by synthetic fiber technology. Products were tested and developed to the point where today's driver, wearing underwear of special resistant materials such as DuPont's Nomex with outer garments of Nomex, glass fiber or other approved material, can survive direct flame contact for over four minutes. Such combinations are now among the requirements.

In addition to the special suits required, drivers must also wear gloves made of leather or Nomex and flame-resistant socks. And, if he has a beard, a driver must wear a face mask of approved material such as Nomex.

In 1960 more specific rules as to the type of lap belt used were incorporated. No longer were the passenger aircraft type of slip-through belts considered adequate. All cars had to be equipped with quick-release, metal-to-metal buckle, three-inch-wide nylon belts, securely fastened through the floorboards to the frame or equally strong mounting points. Some airlines still use the slip-through belt, known to be inferior to mechanical connections.

In 1967 SCCA continued to develop this area of safety by making aircraft-type shoulder harnesses mandatory. These are far better than those seen on production automobiles. A racing harness is a double-strap, over-the-shoulder installation and joins the seat belt at a single quick-release buckle. Required anchorage and installation details cover several paragraphs in the SCCA rule book.

The correctly used shoulder harness is probably the single biggest asset to safety available in the car today. In SCCA, racing injuries to the head, chest and upper extremities were reduced to half of those when shoulder harnesses were not used.

USAC also was quick to move to require full restraint harnesses when it was clear that these would help limit injuries and loss of life. The Grand Prix drivers who came to Indy first rebelled at this, some still preferring to be "thrown clear" in a crash, though this is known to present a far greater hazard. Now most of the top GP racers also use full harnesses in their cars, though they're not compulsory.

With its enclosed stock sedans, NASCAR was able to move faster than other racing associations toward massive roll bar structures that completely surround the driver. These have since set a standard for roll-over protection in auto racing. These roll-over "cages" also add to the stiffness of the car as a whole, a race-preparation technique that's been refined by the builders of Trans-Am cars.

At the end of the Sixties, road racing cars were being equipped, for the first time, with built-in fire extinguishing systems using advanced agents like DuPont's "Freon" FE-1301. Systems of this kind, which allow a driver to start fighting a fire while his car is still moving, were pioneered by Formula 1 Enterprises and adopted by top competitors in the Can-Am Continental and USAC Championship series.

As the technology of racing safety became more complex, and interlinked with new developments in other fields, such as aircraft and production cars, a new organization was formed to bring together specialists in this important area and improve communication between them. Named the Motor Racing Safety Society, it is headquartered at 37 West 57th Street, New York, New York 10019. MRSS works with all the sanctioning bodies, the FIA, the Society of Automotive Engineers and the U.S. Department of Transportation to keep information flowing on all aspects of road racing safety from course design to vehicle dynamics.

Entirely eclipsed in North America for decades, road racing at one time seemed lost beyond recall. But enthusiasts brought it back, men and women who appreciated the art of road racing as practiced in Europe and liked the superbly capable and enjoyable cars it bred. Then came the organizations that were needed to govern a growing sport, and finally the professional people who were required to develop and promote a kind of competition that's caught on from coast to coast.

In its move toward professionalism, road racing hasn't lost its appeal to the club racer who wants to do it for fun. In fact its expansion as a business has made road racing more available than ever before to anyone with a suitable car, the desire to race, and an understanding family, friends or spouse. You may never be able to equal the exploits of a Moss, Donohue or Gurney, but you can practice the same sport they do, and play it on the identical grounds, matching your performance against theirs. What could be more satisfying than that? And you might just turn out to be a star!

GLOSSARY

AAA: American Automobile Association.

AAR: All American Racers. An American racing car building and racing firm, originally founded by Dan Gurney and Carroll Shelby.

ACCUS: Automobile Competition Committee (United States). Affiliation of American auto clubs that represents U.S. sporting interests in FIA activities.

ARCA: Automobile Racing Club of America.

Amateur: Driver or other participant who takes part in automotive competitions solely for personal pleasure.

Anchors: Brakes.

Anti-Roll Bar: See Roll Bar.

Apex: That point in a corner at which the racing car comes closest to the inside edge of the road. A key point in correctly judging one's entry to and departure from a corner.

133

Back Off: Reduce or slacken speed or power.

Ball Joint: Provides movement in any plane, between two members by means of a ball on one and a socket on the other.

Banking: Inward inclination of corners of an oval or circular race track.

Bend: Damage a racing car.

BHP: Brake horsepower. Net power available at the output shaft of the engine. (Brake refers to a measuring device, a dynamometer.)

Big Bangers: Cars with engines of large cylinder displacement.

Binders: Brakes.

Bite: Traction of tires on pavement.

Block: Cylinder-containing element of an internal combustion engine.

Blow: Engine failure.

Blower: Supercharger.

BMW: Bavarian Motor Works, a German auto builder.

Boondocks: Off the course; i.e., "He headed for the boondocks." Also known as Boonies.

Bore: Measurement across the cylinder (diameter).

Box: Transmission.

Brake: 1. Mechanism for slowing and stopping the road wheel. 2. (Also Break) Term (European and English) for Station Wagon.

BRM: British Racing Motor, a British racing car.

Broke: Out of competition due to mechanical failure.

Bucket Seat: Individual seat, often contoured to provide lateral support.

Buy the Farm: To be killed while auto racing.

CC: Cubic centimeters, usually in reference to engine displacement. 1000cc equals one liter.

CI: Cubic inches, usually in reference to engine displacement. Also shown as cu. ins. and CID.

CSI: Commission Sportive Internationale. Rules-making body within FIA.

Cad-Allard: British Allard sports car powered by a Cadillac engine.

Camber: Angle at which the car wheels sit on the roadway.

Can-Am: (SCCA) The Canadian-American Championship for drivers of sports/racing cars.

Charger: Very aggressive driver.

Chassis: 1. Underpart of an automobile, consisting of frame with axles, brakes, wheels, engine, transmission, driveline and exhaust system. 2. Base frame without running gear.

Chicane: Obstacles or barriers added to existing road course to form a tighter turn or series of turns, generally with the objective of reducing average speed.

Circuit: Road course used for conducting automobile races, on which cars repeatedly retrace the same route.

Closed Event: Race for participants only, with paying spectators not admitted.

Club Race: Automobile competition organized by a club for its members and guests. Indicates an amateur event.

Clutch: Coupling for connecting two working parts; i.e., cone clutch, dog clutch, etc.

Cobbled (Cobbled-up): Production car with experimental components added or substituted.

Compression (Compression Ratio): Ratio of uncompressed to compressed volume in an engine cylinder bore.

Compressor: Supercharger.

Con-Rod: Connecting rod. Rod which connects crankshaft and piston in a reciprocating internal combustion engine.

Continental: (SCCA) The Continental Championship for drivers of single-seater racing cars conforming to formulas A and B.

Cool-Off Lap: Extra lap taken at the end of a race to ensure that a sufficient number have been completed and also to permit the engine and working parts to come gradually to a lower temperature.

Cutoff Point: The physical location on the track, before each corner, where the driver takes his foot off the throttle and puts it hard on the brakes. Subject to adjustment according to brake performance and intensity of competition.

DNF: Did not finish. Started a race but failed to complete it.

DNS: Did not start. Properly entered for a race but prevented from appearing at the starting line to begin the event.

DOHC: Double overhead camshaft cylinder head.

De Dion: Reference to designer of De Dion-type rear suspension wherein action of wheels is related through a connecting tube.

Dial In: To make technical adjustments to engine or suspensions, as, "He dialed in closer valve clearances."

Dicing: (British) Close, exciting and highly competitive driving.

Differential: Gear-driven axle assembly which transmits power from drive shaft to wheels. Derived from provision for a different speed of each wheel in a turn.

Displacement: Volume, in cubic measure, of cylinder or engine, not including combustion chamber volume.

Distributor: Mechanism driven by a shaft geared to the camshaft which provides timed electrical impulses to the spark plugs.

Drafting: See Slipstreaming.

Drift: Four-wheel controlled slide, using power to keep car on the road in a corner.

Driver's School: On-course training for drivers. Consists of time trials, supervised novice racing, discussion periods and critiques.

Esses: Winding "S" turns on road racing circuit.

FIA: Fédération Internationale de l'Automobile. International automotive governing body.

FWD: Front-wheel drive; engine and drive axle mounted at front end of chassis.

Flag (s): International racing flags as used in road racing.

Flagman: Marshal responsible for displaying flags at control station on race circuit.

Flat Four: Horizontally opposed four cylinder engine (VW).

Flat Out: Full speed; straining to reach the maximum possible.

Flat Six: Horizontally opposed six cylinder engine (Corvair).

Flip: To overturn, roll over.

Flying Start: Racing start wherein competing cars take starting flag approaching racing speed.

FoMoCo: Ford Motor Car Company or Ford engine or parts.

Formula Libre: Free or open racing organized without reference or conforming to any FIA formula or CSI category.

Formula 1: (1966-1972) Description of Grand Prix championship cars. Up to 3000cc, unsupercharged. Minimum dry weight without ballast, 500 kilograms. Commercial fuel. Self starter obligatory. No oil replenishment during race.

Formula 2: (1967-1971) FIA competition category. 1600cc unsupercharged. Maximum cylinders: 6. Block from production car. Commercial fuel. Minimum dry weight without ballast, 420 kilograms.

Formula 3: FIA competition category providing for competition within the means of private entrants intended to serve as a training ground for future Grand Prix drivers and development of production engines and components.

Four Wheel Drive (4wd): Vehicle with provision for driving all four road wheels.

Fuel Cell: Special container, generally of reinforced rubber, designed to hold fuel and to retain it even when car is damaged, as in a crash.

Full Bore: Full speed; wide-open throttle.

GP (Grand Prix): From the French usage. 1. Race for Formula 1 cars. 2. Designation of a major international road racing event.

GT: See Gran Turismo.

Getting a Tow: See Slipstreaming.

Gran Turismo: (Italian) Closed two-seat coupe designed for rapid, comfortable touring with good performance and handling. (In English, "Grand Touring.")

Grand American: (NASCAR) An event in the Grand American Championship series for drivers of small American stock-based sedans.

Grand National: (NASCAR) An event in the Grand National Championship series for drivers of American stock-based sedans.

Grande Epreuve: (French) Major test, designating a race in which points will be won toward the World Championship for Drivers.

Grid: 1. Alignment for cars at start of race. 2. Start markings on the circuit at the starting line.

Gymkhana: Competition wherein cars execute prescribed driving maneuvers, not one against the other, but against the clock.

Hairpin: Acute corner on road racing circuit.

Hairy: Hair-raising, unusual or extraordinary.

Hemi: Engine with hemispherical combustion chambers.

Hillclimb: Speed competition between cars of one or more classes over a closed hill circuit. Cars compete one at a time against the clock.

History: Broken, wrecked, unusable, as, "That car is history." Also Historied, as, "We historied another engine at Laguna Seca."

Homologation: Procedure by which a car manufacturer guarantees that a particular model is produced in series conforming to FIA rules for a given category; i.e., at least 1000 identical units in 12 months to qualify as a Touring car; at least 100 units in 12 months to qualify as a Grand Touring car.

Hot Shoe: A fast, capable racing driver.

IFS: Independent Front Suspension.

IRS: Independent Rear Suspension.

IMSA: International Motor Sports Association.

Impound Area: Enclosed area to which cars may be required to be taken at the end of a race for inspection to be sure they meet eligibility requirements.

Index: In endurance races, a theoretical calculation of the distance a car should travel in the time period of the race. Actual race performance is compared with the calculation to determine the success of the car in terms of its Index of Performance. Objective is to allow cars of all engine sizes to compete on equal footing.

Koni(s): Trade name for an adjustable, hydraulic strut-type shock absorber.

Lap(s): Complete tour(s) of the race course, track or circuit.

Le Mans Start: Racing start wherein drivers run across the course to their cars, start their engines and depart.

Limited Slip (Sometimes limited slip differential): Mechanism in differential which automatically engages the non-slipping drive wheel when the other loses traction.

Line: 1. The fastest path around a given race course, e.g. the correct line or the best line. 2. The path being followed at any moment by a racing car and driver, as, "He took an unusual line through the corner."

Liter: Metric unit of volumetric measure, 1000 cubic centimeters. Roughly equivalent to a quart or 61 cubic inches.

Lunch an Engine: Destroy an engine.

MG: Originally from Morris Garages, a famous British sporting car.

MPG: Miles Per Gallon. Miles an automobile can cover on one gallon of fuel.

Machine: An automobile, with favorable connotations.

Mag(s): 1. Wheel cast in magnesium, then machined for attachment to hub, etc. Used primarily for racing because of extremely light weight. 2. Magneto(s).

Manifold: Mixture distribution pipes from carburetor to cylinders (inlet); exhaust gas collecting pipes from cylinders to outlet (exhaust).

Marque: (British) Nameplate or make of car.

Marshal: Flagman or communications worker.

Mickey Mouse Circuit: Small, winding race circuit.

Monocoque: Design which unitizes body and chassis into single structure.

Monoposto: Single seat racing car.

MoPar: 1. Chrysler Corporation automobile. 2. Official Chrysler Corporation replacement part.

Mule: 1. A rough cobbled-up prototype of a planned new racing or production car. 2. A car set aside by a racing team for use in practice only, not for an actual race.

NASCAR: National Association for Stock Car Auto Racing.

National: (SCCA) A National Championship event, one of at least six run each year in each of the SCCA's seven racing divisions to determine the best drivers in twenty-one classes of cars.

Non-Speed Event: Includes rallies, concours d'elegance, gymkhanas, etc. Events not requiring special competition licenses.

OHV: Overhead Valve Engine or cylinder head.

OSCA: Officine Specializzate per la Costruzioni di Automobili. Firm in Bologna, Italy, founded by the Maserati brothers to build small racing cars of high quality.

Open-Wheeled: Racing car not required to have fenders or road equipment, hence designed with entirely exposed wheels, as for Indianapolis or Formula 1 racing.

Oval: Oval shape racetrack.

Oversteer: Tendency of car to steer itself increasingly into a corner, requiring driver to reduce steering pressure or to turn the wheel out of the corner. (Opposite of Understeer:)

Pace Car: Vehicle used to pace race cars at flying start.

Paddock: Area, generally adjacent to pits, where competition cars and service vehicles are parked, serviced and prepared.

Paint the Wall: (USAC) To hit the wall or barrier at the outside of a corner, usually involuntarily.

Pit(s): Service stall or area assigned to each car competing in a race.

Pit Lane: Lane in front of pits for entrance and exit of racing cars.

Pit Stop: Stop made at pit by competing car.

Power to Weight Ratio: Ratio of horsepower to weight of car. Most commonly expressed in horsepower per pound.

Protest: An official objection on the basis of race regulations lodged against one competitor by another.

Prototype: 1. Test model of new car. 2. Sports/racing car which does not conform to standards or minimum production requirements for homologated sports cars.

Pump Fuel: Racing fuel of no higher octane rating than that available for sale at gasoline station pumps.

Qualifying: Prerace speed trails held to determine eligibility for an event and/or order of cars and drivers for the start.

RPM: Revolutions Per Minute.

Rack and Pinion: A type of steering mechanism.

Radius Rod (Also Radius Arm): Distance rod, usually mounted on axle to maintain position relative to chassis.

Rain Tire: Tire designed with softer rubber (or mix and tread) to provide greater adhesion on wet road surfaces.

Rally: Organized automobile-run conducted in compliance with applicable motor vehicle laws, designed to test the driving and navigational skills of the contestants. The contestants start from a given point at fixed intervals, with the object of following a prescribed course at specified legal and safe speeds without deviating from scheduled times of arrival at predetermined points along the course unknown to the contestants.

Regional: (SCCA) Lowest level of authorized amateur road racing, organized into Regional Championship events in seven SCCA racing divisions.

Revs: Engine revolutions per minute.

Road Race: Motor race staged on a road or simulated road course.

Roadster: 1. Open two-seater car with light-duty weather protection. 2.

Nickname of typical Indy car of 1953-63 in which driver sat low alongside the drive shaft.

Roll Bar(s): 1. Safety bar(s) that protects driver. 2. Sway or anti-roll bar, for suspension control.

Rookie: (USAC) Driver who is a member of the starting field for the first time in the Indianapolis 500-Mile Race.

Runner: Vehicle in the competition.

SCCA: Sports Car Club of America.

SOHC: Single Overhead Camshaft engine or cylinder head.

Sandbagging: Practicing or qualifying for a race at a speed deliberately lower than that of which the car and driver are capable.

Scrutineering: (British) Detailed technical inspection to assess raceworthiness or conformity to competing cars.

Shock(s): Shock absorber(s), used to damp out suspension movements.

Shunt: Accident, involving a crash.

Shut the Gate: To block or move into another driver's line.

Slipstreaming: Driving very close to tail of another racing car to take advantage of resulting decreased wind resistance.

Space Frame: Chassis frame built of multiple tubes.

Spoiler: Air deflector used on cars to control lift tendencies.

Sports Car: A car of taut, responsive and precise handling qualities and possessed of sprightly performance. A car which can serve as an extension of the driver's sensibilities. Must also be able to be equipped to be registered for highway use.

Sporty Car: Automobile designed to give the impression that it is a sports car but in reality is not.

Stand On It: 1. To step all the way down on the throttle pedal. 2. To race aggressively.

Standing Start: Start of a race from a stationary grid, cars at rest with engines running and drivers in position.

Start: Beginning of a race.

Starter: Marshal who controls the master flag at the start/finish line. The chief starter.

Start/Finish: The line that serves (in nearly all cases) as the place on the circuit where a race starts and finishes. (Notable exceptions are the Sebring 12 Hours and Daytona 24 Hours, where these lines are in two different places.)

Stock: Unmodified car conforming to certain strict specifications, as opposed to modified cars.

Stroke: 1. Distance piston travels in cylinder bore. 2. To drive to plan, lower than maximum speed.

Supercharger: A mechanical device which increases an engine's power by forcing air into its cylinders at a pressure higher than that exerted by the atmosphere.

Synch (Synchromesh): Device for synchronizing gears to eliminate clash or grinding when gear shifts are made.

Tach (Tachometer): Instrument which measures engine speed in revolutions per minute.

Teardown: Disassembly of car or engine components to verify that engine size and other specifications meet the racing class requirements.

Tech Inspection: See Scrutineering.

Time Trials: 1. Speed competition on closed course with each car running against the clock only for fastest time. 2. Timed practice laps to determine starting position on grid.

Torque: Force which produces or tends to produce torsion or rotation. The turning power of a shaft or engine.

Torsion Bar: Rod so fixed in a suspension system that it serves as a spring. One end is anchored to the chassis frame, the other to the suspension. Wheel movement (up or down) causes rod to rotate or twist.

Tow (also Getting a Tow): See Slipstreaming.

Track: Race Course.

Trans-Am: (SCCA) The Trans-American Championship for makers of medium-sized and small sedans.

Transaxle: Transmission and rear axle mounted in unit at the rear of the chassis.

Transmission: Gearbox. Automatic or manual gear changing mechanism used to apply engine power to road wheels according to demand.

Tweak (also Tweaking): Mild forms of engine modification to increase power output.

Understeer: Tendency of car to steer itself increasingly out of a corner, requiring added steering effort of the driver. (Opposite of Oversteer.)

USAC: United States Auto Club.

"V": Engine design; i.e., V4, V6, V8, V12, or V16. Indicates that cylinder bores form an angle of less than 180 degrees, i.e., 90-degree V8.

VSCCA: Vintage Sports Car Club of America.

Watt Linkage: A suspension linkage which provides vertical wheel hub movement. Named for its innovator.

Weber(s): Carburetors designed and manufactured by Edoardo Weber of Turin, Italy.

Weight Distribution: Distribution of weight in a motor vehicle front to rear, at the axles.

INDEX

144

Richardson, Claude D., Jr., 19
Riley, Art, 35
Rindt, Jochen, 36, 105, 108, 113, 114, 115
Roberts, Fireball, 35
Rodriguez, Pedro, 24, 25, 53, 90, 112
Rosemeyer, Bernd, 102
Ruby, Lloyd, 25, 28, 95, 97
Rudkin, Hank, 67
Rutan, Bill, 35
Ruttman, Troy, 89

Sanborn, Nils, 71
Savage, Swede, 30, 33, 35, 83, 99
Scarfiotti, Ludovico, 53
Schell, Harry, 104, 106
Schenken, Tim, 69
Scott, Bill, 66, 71
Sell, Lou, 79-80
Sharp, Hap, 25, 50, 52
Shelby, Carroll, 20, 23, 25, 38, 41
Siffert, Jo, 27, 112
Smith, George M., 63-64
Smith, Reggie, 19, 36
Smith, Robert, 71
Smothers, Dick, 75
Snell, Peter, 130
Snively, George S., 130
Southgate, Tony, 79
Spear, Bill, 47
Spence, Mike, 23, 26
Sports Car Club of America, Inc. (SCCA), 5-15, 21, 31, 36, 43-44, 46, 49, 57, 60, 63, 68, 70, 71, 74, 76, 89, 98, 99, 118, 119, 126
classifications, 11-12
helmet specifications, 127, 130
safety equipment, 129-131
school program, 126-128
Stevenson, Fred, 84
Stewart, Jackie, 105, 114, 115
Stroppe, Bill, 32

Surtees, John, 25, 52, 53, 86, 100, 103, 107, 112, 113, 115
Swanson, Carl, 10
Sweikert, Bob, 87

Taruffi, Piero, 23
Terry, Len, 79, 82
Thomas, Bill, 32
Thompson, Mickey, 51
Tinglestad, Bud, 93
Titus, Jerry, 38, 41
Tolan, Johnnie, 89
Tomaso, Alejandro de, 106
Troutman, Dick, 49
Tullius, Bob, 14, 36, 38
Turner, Curtis, 32, 35, 36

Ulmann, Alexander Edward, 19, 20, 25, 35, 104, 106
Ulmann, Mary, 19, 20, 104
United States Auto Club (USAC), 6, 7, 32, 34, 50, 85, 87, 89, 92, 93, 94, 95, 97, 98, 99, 119, 131
Unser, Al, 88, 95, 96, 97, 98, 99
Unser, Bobby, 86, 91, 94, 95, 96, 97, 98
Unser, Louie, 83

Wacker, Fred, 19
Walker, David, 70
Walker, Rob, 107
Walters, Phil, 18, 20
Ward, Rodger, 90, 92-93, 99, 106
Watson, A. J., 93
Weaver, George, 76
Wilke, Bob, 106
Williams, Frank, 114
Williams, Jonathan, 53
Wintersteen, George, 75, 79, 81
Women, road racing and, 4-5
Wyer, John, 26, 27, 28

Zink, Ed, 66